LEMONGRASS
AND SWEET BASIL
TRADITIONAL THAI CUISINE

LEMONGRASS
AND SWEET BASIL

TRADITIONAL THAI CUISINE

by Khamtane Signavong
photography by Ken Martin and Alison Plummer

Interlink Books

An imprint of Interlink Publishing Group, Inc.
Northampton, Massachusetts

Dedication
In memory of our good friend
Chirawat Siripongvirush

First published in 2005 by

INTERLINK BOOKS
An imprint of Interlink Publishing Group, Inc.
46 Crosby Street, Northampton, Massachusetts 01060
www.interlinkbooks.com

PB: ISBN 1 56656-626-6

Reproduction by Pica Digital PTE Ltd, Singapore
Printed and bound by Times Offset (M) Sdn. Bhd., Malaysia

2 4 6 8 10 9 7 5 3 1

To request our complete 40-page full-color catalog,
please call us toll-free at **1-800-238-LINK**,
visit our website at **www.interlinkbooks.com**, or write to
Interlink Publishing
46 Crosby Street, Northampton, MA 01060
e-mail: info@interlinkbooks.com

contents

Introduction

Being Thai is a way of life, from our Thai Buddhist religion to the customs and traditions passed down through generations. Food plays a very large role in our day-to-day living—you could say we have a passion for eating—but there is more involved than merely satisfying our taste buds. The importance of the process of preparation, care in presentation, the essential balance of flavors, as well as the spiritual significance of food, are all part of what might be called the whole "Thainess" of the experience, whether the meal features the elaborate detail of Royal Thai Cuisine (so-called because in the past this type of cooking was prepared in the Palace's Inner Court and served only to royals and artistocrats) or is a simple snack from a street stall.

Every day at dawn in Thailand, monks in saffron-colored robes file out from their monasteries and *wats* (temples) carrying their alms bowls, which are filled by people who wait to give them food, especially precious rice (*khao*), which is at the heart of Thai life. We don't give alms every day but do so as often as possible, wherever we are in the world. The idea is, loosely, that giving the best of what you have to the monks and to your elders and guests will earn you spiritual brownie points—and food is a valuable part of the currency.

After the initial greeting (men say *sawadee khap*, women say *sawadee kha*), the next thing that Thais will say, before any further words are exchanged, is "Have you eaten yet?" The time of day doesn't make any difference to the Thai desire to offer you food, and I think that Western people may find this strange. Thais have no set mealtimes, often eating about five times a day, enjoying single dishes and snacks as well as main meals. We love to eat in groups, sharing dishes that combine to make a properly balanced meal and incorporate the four vital flavor characteristics of Thai food—spicy, salty, sweet, and sour. Understanding this balance is the first step toward creating Thai dishes yourself.

Evening at Wat Phra That Doi Suthep near Chiang Mai.

Here are the basic ingredients we use to achieve the famous four Ss.

Spicy—chiles, bell peppers, fresh and dried spices, shallots, garlic.

Salty—fish sauce, soy sauce, dried shrimp, shrimp paste, salt.

Sweet—coconut milk, palm sugar, fruit.

Sour—lime juice, tamarind, vinegar, vegetables.

What to cook is the next decision, and Thai meals differ from those in Western countries in that they typically include several dishes to share:

Rice
Curry
Soup
Salad
Stir-fry
Dipping sauce with fresh or steamed vegetables
Broiled or grilled meat, poultry, or fish
Chiles with fish sauce
Iced water

The recipes in this book are intended to serve four people as part of a Thai meal—in a restaurant four people would order four different dishes or more, depending on how hungry they are and how much they can afford. The dishes are always placed in the center of the table, to share, so everyone has a reasonable amount of everything. More dishes are ordered as necessary.

The number of dishes ordered works out at roughly one per person, and rice is always central to the meal. At the restaurant, we have a Western-style menu with appetizers, soups, main courses, and desserts listed individually. At home, you can serve courses separately, because I realize that soup served with a main course is not usual. Noodles, such as the famous *pad thai* noodles, may be served on their own, and Thai snacks (*khap klaem*) served with drinks are also separate from a main meal.

My mother used to tell me that when you cook, you must ensure you buy the best, freshest ingredients and the right quantity of food to go around. She also taught me that chiles, palm sugar, fish sauce, and shrimp paste are all seasonal, and that their taste and heat also depend on the brands you buy, which will vary in the amount of salt and chiles they include. One thing people often ask is whether all Thai dishes have to be hot and spicy by definition. The answer is that not all are, but because we love chiles and spices so much, I recommend that you use them to taste. Leaving them out altogether would upset the fine balance of the recipe.

I grew up with a mother and grandmother who went to the markets every morning, buying everything fresh for the day's meals in the traditional Thai way. At night, we would all go to the markets for mangoes, sticky rice, desserts, and fruit. Now that I

Chili dipping sauces are served with steamed or fresh vegetables.

am running a restaurant, it is my turn to go around the markets in order to select the best local produce.

For daily shopping, go with an open mind as Thais have always done, searching the markets for fresh produce such as meat, seafood, and fresh vegetables, and looking out for seasonal specials. Of course, you must plan ahead for special occasions, and Thais like to be prepared, always having their own herb gardens growing chiles, lemongrass, a lime tree, kaffir limes, galangal, mint, basil, shallots, cilantro, and everything they possibly can for absolute freshness.

Thais are lucky because Thailand is incredibly rich in food resources, with a climate so suitable for growing rice that a harvest is possible twice a year. Because of the abundance of water in the Central and Northern regions, many fruits and vegetables are grown, including cool-climate varieties such as asparagus, strawberries, and snow peas. River shrimp and river fish are plentiful, as well as seafood from Thailand's long coastlines, and shrimp and fish farms export their produce worldwide. The ingredients used in this book are available around the world—a few may take some tracking down through specialty suppliers, but you will find them.

You will notice in the regional sections that many influences have come to bear on Thai cooking, from the cuisine and techniques of the Royal Palace to those from neighboring Laos, Cambodia, Myanmar, and Malaysia. The exchanges of culture and trade between Thailand and these countries bordering it have helped Thailand to raise its standard of living. Traders introduced spices, and Chinese immigrants arriving in the eighteenth and nineteenth centuries brought noodles and bean sprouts, together with techniques such as stir-frying, steaming, and roasting. These cooking skills laid the foundations of Central regional cooking. If Thai food has been slow to make

Selecting fresh produce at the Chiang Mai morning markets.

its name around the world, I think it may be because the country has never been colonized as the French did Vietnam, the Dutch Indonesia, or the British India.

Thai food is now known and appreciated around the world, and I am happy to share some ideas for recipes with you from our kitchens at the Arun Thai in Sydney. As is the case in most cultures, Thais learn their cooking skills from their elders, and so the techniques come easily.

After a time, you will develop your own Thai taste, knowing how to add more or less of the four Ss— spicy, salty, sweet, and sour—to create the right flavor for the right dish.

Ingredients

Bamboo shoots *(Nor mai)*
Fresh, young bamboo shoots should be peeled and sliced prior to cooking. If you use canned bamboo shoots, you should drain them and boil them for about 5 minutes in fresh water. Otherwise, they are likely to have a tangy, metallic taste.

Preserved or pickled bamboo shoots *(Nor mai dong)*
Mostly used in red and Southern yellow curries *(gaeng leung)*, preserved or pickled bamboo shoots come in jars, preserved in vinegar, and should be washed thoroughly in cold water before use.

Banana *(Gluay)*
Many varieties of banana are grown all over Thailand. We use sugar bananas for desserts and deep-fry them for banana chips.

Banana blossom or banana flower *(Hua pee)*
This is the large bud at the end of the banana plant. Only the inside is used. Banana blossoms are available, either fresh or preserved, at specialty Asian grocery shops. Only a stainless steel knife should be used to cut fresh banana blossoms, because any other metal causes discoloration. Do not prepare more than half an hour in advance. Soak preserved banana blossoms in cold water and rinse before use.

Banana leaf *(Bai dthong)*
Thais use banana leaves to wrap food for steaming and broiling, and for wrapping up desserts such as sticky rice with banana. Before the introduction of the plastic bag, banana leaves were used for carrying fresh food.

Basil
Thai sweet basil differs from other types of basil and is worth seeking out—or growing—to add an authentic Thai flavor to many dishes. If Thai, holy, or lemon basil are unavailable, substitute the more widely available Mediterranean variety.

Holy basil *(Bai kaprow—L. Ocinum sanctum)*
Pungent, spicy, aromatic, and fragrant with reddish-purple hairy stems. Only the leaves are used in dishes such as jungle curries and beef, chicken, or lamb stir-fries.

Lemon basil *(Bai manglak—L.Ocinum basilicum "Citriodorum")*
This is a lighter green than Thai sweet basil and is not used as much as the other two varieties except in Northern regional cuisine and Isan recipes.

Thai sweet basil *(Bai horapa L. Ocinum basilicum "Thai")*
Thai sweet basil, available from Asian markets or specialty shops, has leaves that are deep green and smaller than European sweet basil *(L. Ocinum basilicum)*. You can distinguish Thai sweet basil by its purplish stems and purple-tinged flower buds. It is mixed in at the very end of the cooking stage, to bring out its sweet aniseed flavor. Thai sweet basil can be grown anywhere that has direct, warm sunlight—a summer garden, sunny balcony, kitchen windowsill, or greenhouse.

Bean curd *(see Tofu page 13)*

Beans *(Thao fa yao)*
The green beans in Thai cooking are usually the variety known as snake beans or sometimes yard-long beans. They are used in stir-fries, dipping sauces, and salads. Green beans may be used instead.

Bean sprouts *(Tua noork)*
Sprouted from green mung beans, fresh bean sprouts are added to noodle dishes, salads, soups, and stir-fries.

Betel leaf *(Bai cha puu)*
Known as betel leaf, although not from the actual betel tree, these leaves grow on a low bush and are used for wrapping ingredients. They can also be cut up and added to curries. They are also known as wild pepper. Chinese broccoli (see opposite) can be substituted.

Bitter melon *(Mara)*
A bitter-tasting, gourdlike fruit with bumpy, blistered skin. It is used when a true bitter taste is called for in recipes for soups and stir-fries. Bitter melon can also be eaten raw with dipping sauces.

Chiles *(Prik)*
Used for their color as well as their fragrance and spicy, dynamic heat, chiles, originally introduced to Thailand by Portuguese traders, feature prominently in Thai recipes. You will find a heat rating for each recipe with the serving information. Many different varieties are grown all over the world, varying in size, color, and heat; Thai chiles are especially aromatic and fragrant. The two we use most are the bird's eye chiles for heat and sky-pointing chiles for color. In Thailand, bird's eye chiles are some of the hottest available. It is important to carry out a "test run" for all Thai recipes, especially if you are entertaining, in order to gauge the chile temperature you might achieve—which will still be by trial and error, depending on where the chiles are

grown. Generally speaking, the smaller the chile the greater its heat, but this is not always the case! Seeding chiles reduces their heat a little: wear rubber gloves to do this. Never touch your eyes after handling chiles and wash your hands thoroughly after doing so.

Banana chile *(Prik yuak)*
Mild and yellowish green in color, the banana chile measures up to 5½ in (14 cm) in length.

Bird's eye chile *(Prik khi nu)*
This is a tiny chile, measuring up to ¾ in (2 cm) in length. The Thai name means "mouse dropping," which accurately describes its size. These are the hottest of all chiles.

Sky-pointing chile *(Prik chi fa)*
These chiles are red, green, or yellow and measure up to 3¼ in (8 cm) in length. They are often seeded prior to use.

Yellow chile *(Prik leung)*
A mild yellow chile used mainly to add color to sauces.

Chili sauce *(Prik or Sriracha sauce)*
This famous chili sauce comes from the Sriracha area on the coastline south of Bangkok. Made with vinegar, garlic, chiles, and salt, it is added to dishes such as Thai omelets, oysters, and sun-dried beef. For the recipe, see page 139.

Dried chiles *(Prik haeng)*
These are whole, sun-dried chiles. Use the large ones for color, the small ones for heat.

Roasted chili paste *(Nam prik pow)*
One of the most important ingredients in recipes from the Central region, this is a combination of shrimp paste, dried hot red chiles, garlic, shallots, tamarind juice, and palm sugar with seasoning, used in the famous *Tom Yum Goong* soup (see pages 24–25), Banana Flower Salad (see pages 28–29) and some stir-fries. For the recipe, see page 14.

Chinese broccoli *(Kana)*
Also known as Chinese kale, Chinese broccoli has oval leaves on a long, thin stalk. It is used in stir-fries and as a substitute for betel leaves.

Chinese cabbage *(Pak kad kao)*
Chinese cabbage has thin, crinkly leaves and a thick, white stalk. It is used in soups and stir-fries, and can be steamed to serve with a dipping sauce. It is also used to wrap fish prior to steaming, to prevent the fish from sticking to the plate in the steamer.

Chinese chives *(Kui chi)*
These have flat leaves and a garlic flavor. Use in *pad thai* noodles and for garnishing.

Cilantro *(Pak chee)*
This is a fragrant member of the parsley family. Thais use the whole cilantro plant—leaves, stems, seeds, roots, and all. The leaves and stalks are for flavoring, while the roots are used to flavor marinades and stocks. The seeds are used in curries and in marinades for some meat dishes.

Cloud ear fungus *(Hed hunuu)*
Also known as wood or black fungus, cloud ear fungus grows throughout Asia and is available fresh or dried. It is used in soups, jungle curries, and salad. Look for it dried in Asian grocery stores—it should be soaked in warm water for 30 minutes before using. Field mushrooms may be substituted.

Coconut milk *(Kathi)*
This is a must in many delicious Thai curries, especially those from the Central region, and is also a key ingredient in many Thai desserts. Coconut milk and concentrated coconut cream *(hua kathi)* are made from the ripe flesh of the coconut, which is mixed with warm water and squeezed to form coconut cream. After more water is added, the second press produces coconut milk. (See page 16.)

Dried shrimp *(Goong haeng)*
Tiny shrimp from the sea off the coasts of Southern Thailand are sun-dried and used to add a salty, fishy flavor to dishes including *pad thai* noodles, salads, and soups. They are also used in stocks and to make Roasted Chili Paste (see left and page 14).

Squid and anchovies drying in the sun at Rayong.

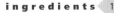

Eggplants (Makeua)

There are many varieties of eggplant, including baby eggplants, which have a bitter taste, and crispy eggplants the size of golf balls, both used in green curries and with *nam prik* dipping sauce. Long eggplants and purple eggplants are used in stir-fries and salads, and, if small or crispy eggplants are unavailable, they can be used in green chicken curries. Pea eggplants (*makeua puong*) or cherry eggplants are the size of large peas and come in bunches. Slightly bitter and crunchy, they give curry an extra texture. Thai eggplants (*makeua piao*) are the size of golf balls, crunchy in texture, but less bitter than pea eggplants.

Fish sauce (Nam pla)

An essential ingredient in Thai cooking, fish sauce is made from small fish, such as anchovies or shrimp, fermented in brine. Fish sauce adds a distinctive salty taste to most Thai dishes, but some brands have extra salt added, which can create an imbalance in the flavors. Look for those brands that are lower in salt.

Galangal (Kha)

An important ingredient in Isan cooking, young, pink-skinned, ribbed galangal rhizomes have white flesh and a distinctly exotic, fragrant, aromatic, and peppery taste—great for soups. As galangal ages, the skin darkens and the flavor becomes stronger, making it good for curry pastes.

Garlic (Kratiam)

Thai garlic is smaller, more pungent, and more fragrant than the larger garlic found in other countries, but is not readily available outside Asia. Use the freshest garlic you can find locally for cooking Thai food.

Pickled garlic (Kratiam dong)

Garlic pickled in vinegar, salt, and sugar is used by Thais as a sauce and condiment.

Ginger (Khing)

Older gingerroots are used for steamed dishes and stir-fries, and younger gingerroots for pickling. The white flowers are eaten with dipping sauce. See also Lesser Ginger, right.

Kaffir lime (Bai magrood)

Both the skin of this knobbly lime (the zest of an ordinary lime can be substituted) and its distinctive figure-of-eight leaves are used. The leaves are thinly sliced or torn to add their strong citrus flavor to soups, stir-fries, and curries. Dried kaffir lime leaves may be used—double the quantity of fresh leaves required and soak for 15–20 minutes in warm water before using. See also Lime, right.

Lemongrass (Takrai)

A stalky grass with a wonderful lemon flavor and fragrance, the outer part is peeled off and only the firm white part inside used. This is crushed for soups, sliced for salads, and pounded for curries. Pounding and crushing releases the fragrant oils from these seemingly dry stalks.

Lesser ginger (Krachai)

Krachai is used to add a gingery and spicy flavor to curried dishes and, like galangal and kaffir lime (see left), is a good foil for strong-flavored meats and seafood. Fresh *krachai* has fingerlike tubers, brown on the outside and pale yellow inside. Preserved *krachai* is available from Asian grocery stores—it should be rinsed well in cold water before using.

Lime (Manao)

One of the main ingredients in Thai cooking, lime gives the sharp, citrus, "sour" Thai taste in soups, salads, and dipping sauces. See also Kaffir lime, left.

Mango (Mamuang)

Many varieties of mango are found in Thailand, each varying in size and taste. Hard, unripe green mangoes are peeled and sliced to give a deliciously sour tang to salads and dipping sauces, while ripe mangoes are eaten as a fruit or as a dessert with sticky rice.

Mint (Bai salanae)

Thai mint has a small, round leaf and a pungent flavor. Garden mint can be substituted.

Mushrooms (Hed)

Mushrooms used in Thai cooking include the small-capped, long-stalked, sweet straw mushroom used in *Tom Yum Goong* soup (see pages 24–25) and stir-fries. Button mushrooms can be substituted for straw mushrooms.

Noodles

Thais eat plenty of noodles, cooked in a variety of ways:

Cellophane or glass noodles (Wun sen)

These are made from mung bean flour and are used in soups, salads, and spring rolls.

Dried rice noodles (Guay teow)

These noodles come in three sizes: large noodles (*sen yai*); medium or rice stick (*sen lek*), like Italian tagliatelle, often used in *pad thai* noodles and noodle soup; and tiny, fine noodles (*sen mee*), like Italian vermicelli, used in noodle soup.

Egg noodles (Ba mee)

Made with all-purpose flour, egg, and water, they are medium flat (*sen ban*) or small and fine (*sen ba mee* or *sen bpan*).

Fresh rice noodles (Kanom jin)

These are served with a selection of sauces and vegetables.

Oil (Nam mun)
Animal fat is traditionally used for cooking in Thailand, but more health-conscious Thais are now switching to vegetable oils.

Oyster sauce (Nam mun hoi)
Made from oyster extract, this sauce has a rich, salty, sweet flavor and a smooth texture. It is mostly used in stir-fries or marinades.

Palm sugar (Nam tan peep)
This is made from the sap of the coconut or sugar palm and varies from dark brown to almost white. Palm sugar is used to balance dishes and add a sharp sweetness.

Pandanus leaf (Bai toey)
Pandanus grows profusely in Thailand and its leaves are widely used in Royal Thai Cuisine to wrap chicken. The fragrant, almost perfumed vanilla flavor goes very well with coconut for desserts. The leaves are inedible and should be discarded before serving.

Papaya (Ma la kor)
There are several varieties of papaya in Thailand, with either long or round fruit. The crispy, crunchy green variety that never ripens is shredded for salads in the North and Isan, while in the South it is used in *Gaeng Leung*. Ripe papaya is eaten on its own and is also dried for use in snacks.

Peppercorns (Prik thai oan)
Unripe green peppercorns are used in jungle curries and stir-fries to help to balance the flavors. Ground white pepper is widely used, while black pepper is only used in some regional dishes.

Pomelo (Som o)
A member of the grapefruit family, the pomelo is a great favorite in salads and is also eaten on its own.

Rice (Khao)
Thailand is the home of fragrant, long-grain jasmine rice (*khao horm mali*), which is highly regarded as the staple for most Thai meals throughout Thailand. Sticky or glutinous rice (*khao niaw*) is eaten instead of jasmine rice in the North and Isan regions. Elsewhere, it is used in desserts such as the famous sticky rice with mango. Ground, roasted rice is rice that has been dry-fried in a wok with galangal until golden brown, then ground to a fine powder and used in many Isan and Northern regional dishes.

Scallions (Ton hom)
Long, green-stemmed scallions are mild in flavor and used in stir-fries, salads, and soups.

Shallots (Hom deng)
Thai shallots are reddish-purple in color and are smaller than brown shallots, which can also be used in Thai recipes. Shallots bring out the flavors in curries, curry pastes, including Roasted Chili Paste (see page 14), and dipping sauces. They are also sliced and used in salads.

Shrimp paste (Gapi)
Pungent and salty, this is a must-have ingredient in curry paste for its aromatic and preserving qualities. It is made from shrimp mixed with salt, which are dried in the sun, then blended to a paste. Used in curries, dipping sauces, and stir-fries, you can find it in Asian grocery stores.

Soy sauce (Nam siew)
Made from fermented soya beans, light soy sauce is salty and aromatic and is used in stir-fries and for soups and marinades; dark soy sauce is sweet and less salty and is used in noodle dishes and some Chinese-influenced dishes.

Tamarind (Mak kam)
Growing in bunches of pods on the tamarind tree, the fruit is crushed and can be bought pressed in block form or as concentrated tamarind paste. Both can be mixed with water to make tamarind juice, see pages 16–17.

Tofu (Bean curd) (Taohu)
Made from the liquid of crushed soya beans, tofu, also known as bean curd, is high in protein and is available either firm or soft. Soft (or silken) bean curd is used in soups or for steaming and roasting. The firm type is good for stir-frying and deep-frying because it keeps its shape while it cooks. Individual recipes specify which kind to use.

Turmeric (Khamin)
A root similar to ginger, turmeric is used for its yellow color as well as its flavor, especially in Southern Thai regional dishes. You can use fresh turmeric root or the more widely available ground turmeric.

Twisted or stink beans (Sator)
These large, flat bitter beans are very popular in Southern Thailand. They are served boiled for dipping or used in stir-fries with shrimp and shrimp paste.

Wing beans (Tua phuu)
Grown in Southeast Asia, these distinctive green beans have a smooth skin with four prominent ridges—when sliced through, each piece is star-shaped. Wing beans are generally used in salads and blanched whole in boiling water to eat with dipping sauces. These beans must be fresh—ask about them in specialty stores.

methods & techniques

Chili curry pastes

Red and green curry pastes are used as a basis for many Thai dishes, while other pastes are individually blended to create specific dishes such as a Mussaman Beef Curry (see pages 114–115). This preblending of herbs and spices is the significant flavor factor in much Thai cooking.

Made from fresh and dried herbs and spices, each recipe is different, depending on the cook and the house style, because each household has its own recipes that are passed on from generation to generation. Thais can tell how good you are at making chili paste by the sound of the mortar and pestle as you pound. Historically, wives were selected on their ability to make good chili paste, but now society has changed and, like families the world over, many Thai households buy paste from supermarkets.

You can do that, too, but passionate cooks will not be content without some recipes. You can either make your paste fresh each time or make a quantity and store it if you intend to cook Thai food often. It keeps—stored in an airtight, sterilized jar—for up to 3 months in the refrigerator. To sterilize the jar, wash it thoroughly in warm, soapy water, rinse, and dry in a moderate oven for 5 minutes.

You can use an electric coffee grinder kept specifically for spices, a food processor, or a blender, but the traditional pounding method is best for the real Thai taste. Fresh ingredients make all the difference when you pound; the idea is to release the moist juices in order to form the paste.

When you cook with coconut milk and curry paste, you aromatize them by heating until the oil separates and floats to the top before adding other ingredients. Dry seeds such as cumin and coriander are toasted by heating a wok and dry-frying the seeds until they change color.

The recipes make about 2–4 tablespoons of paste.

Roasted chili paste
nam prik pao
4 tablespoons vegetable oil
15 cloves garlic, peeled and chopped
5 shallots, peeled and chopped
5 dried red chiles, seeded and soaked in warm water
1 teaspoon shrimp paste
1 tablespoon palm sugar
1 tablespoon tamarind juice (see pages 16–17)
1½ teaspoons salt

Heat the oil in a wok over medium heat, add the garlic and shallots, and fry until golden brown. Remove from the heat and set aside.

Add the chiles and fry until brown. In a mortar, pound the chiles, garlic, shallots, and shrimp paste until fine and return to the wok along with the palm sugar, tamarind juice, and salt. Stir-fry over low heat until the mixture has aromatized and thickened. This paste can be kept in a jar for up to 3 months; top up with vegetable oil to prevent drying.

Gaeng hanglay paste
nam prik gaeng hanglay
1 tablespoon shrimp paste
5 shallots, unpeeled
4 garlic cloves, unpeeled
2 lemongrass stalks, very thinly sliced
1 tablespoon coriander seeds
1 tablespoon cumin seeds
5 large dried chiles, seeded and soaked in warm water
1 teaspoon ground turmeric
½ teaspoon salt

Preheat the oven or broiler to 325°F/160°C. Wrap the shrimp paste in foil, place on a baking sheet with the shallots, garlic and lemongrass, and bake for 10 minutes. Set aside to cool, then peel off the skins.

In a wok, dry-fry the coriander and cumin seeds over medium heat until dark brown and fragrant, about 5 minutes. Put the baked ingredients, dry-fried seeds, chiles, turmeric, and salt into a mortar and pound to a fine paste.

Chiang mai noodle paste
nam prik gaeng khao soi
5 dried bird's eye chiles, seeded and soaked in warm water
1 lemongrass stalk
3 shallots, peeled and sliced
2 slices of galangal
2 kaffir lime leaves
½ teaspoon ground turmeric
1 teaspoon grated kaffir (or ordinary) lime zest
5 garlic cloves, peeled and chopped
1 teaspoon coriander seeds

Combine all the ingredients in a mortar and pound to a paste with a pestle. Use a blender if you prefer.

Green curry paste
nam prik gaeng khao wan
1 teaspoon coriander seeds
½ teaspoon cumin seeds
10 green bird's eye chiles or green chiles, chopped
1 stalk lemongrass, finely sliced
2 shallots, peeled and chopped
1 teaspoon sliced galangal
1 teaspoon chopped cilantro root
1 tablespoon ground black pepper
2 tablespoons sliced kaffir lime leaves
½ teaspoon grated kaffir lime zest
1 teaspoon shrimp paste
1 teaspoon salt

Toast the dry seeds in a wok and then grind them until fine in a mortar and pestle. Now, put the remaining ingredients into the mortar and pound with a pestle until you achieve a paste.

Red curry paste
nam prik gaeng phet
1 teaspoon shrimp paste
1 tablespoon coriander seeds
½ teaspoon cumin seeds
15 big dried chiles, seeded and soaked in warm water
1 lemongrass stalk, finely sliced
2 teaspoons chopped shallots
1 garlic clove, minced
1 teaspoon grated galangal
1 tablespoon freshly ground black pepper
2 kaffir lime leaves, sliced
½ teaspoon kaffir lime zest, finely chopped
1 teaspoon salt

Wrap the shrimp paste in foil and broil for 5 minutes. Toast and grind the dry seeds. Blend all the ingredients together to a paste using either a mortar and pestle or a food processor.

Panang curry paste
nam prik panang
1 tablespoon shrimp paste
1 tablespoon coriander seeds
½ tablespoon cumin seeds
15 big dried red chiles, seeded and soaked in warm water
2 tablespoons shallots, chopped
3 tablespoons chopped garlic
1 lemongrass stalk, finely sliced
1 teaspoon galangal, sliced
1 tablespoon chopped cilantro root
3 tablespoons freshly toasted mung beans, crushed

Wrap the shrimp paste in foil and broil for 5 minutes. Toast the seeds, then blend everything together in a mortar, using a pestle to form a fine paste.

Mussaman curry paste
nam prik gaeng mussaman

1 teaspoon coriander seeds
2 cardamom pods
1 teaspoon black peppercorns
1 teaspoon cumin seeds
1 nutmeg
2 cloves
6 big dried red chiles, seeded and soaked in
  water
4 garlic cloves, peeled and finely chopped
3 shallots, peeled and finely chopped
6 slices of galangal, finely chopped
1 lemongrass stalk, finely chopped
1 teaspoon shrimp paste
2 teaspoons vegetable oil
1 teaspoon salt

Heat the wok over low heat and add the coriander seeds, cardamom, black pepper, cumin, nutmeg, and cloves and dry stir-fry until fragrant, about 4–5 minutes. Remove and set aside to cool. Using the same wok, stir-fry all the remaining ingredients (except the shrimp paste, oil, and salt) until fragrant, then remove and set aside to cool.

Put all the spices in a mortar and pound to a fine paste with the pestle. Add all the remaining ingredients and continue to pound to a fine paste. This paste can be stored in a jar in the refrigerator for up to 3 months.

Coconut milk
Coconut milk and coconut cream are available in cans or packages. Coconut milk is the squeezed white flesh of the coconut mixed with hot water. The first pressing produces coconut cream, and the second produces thinner milk. Buy them individually or separate the cream from a can of coconut milk; when you open it, you will find the dense cream floating on the top of the milk. If you want to make coconut milk at home: 2¼ cups (225 g) shredded (or dry unsweetened) coconut mixed with 2½ cups (600 ml) water produces 2 cups (450 ml) coconut milk.

Rice
The cooking time and amount of water required depend on the age of the rice used. Very white rice is generally new and more moist, so it needs less water. Older rice is more yellow in color and is harder, so it needs more water.

Jasmine rice—my grandmother rinsed the long-grain jasmine rice three times in fresh water before putting it into a saucepan and covering it with water. The traditional Thai way of measuring is to place your hand flat over the rice and to add enough water to cover both. Cook from cold, bringing the water to a boil for 7 minutes, then simmering until all the water is absorbed, about 15–20 minutes in total.

Sticky or glutinous rice is soaked overnight before cooking, usually by steaming for about 20 minutes. Quantities are always hard to gauge, but as a rule 1¾ cups (400 g) jasmine rice in 4½ cups (1 liter) cold water serves four, depending on your appetite. Rice is central to a meal in Thailand, and so we always have plenty on hand. Electric rice cookers are used widely in Thailand.

Shredded pork skin
Buy 7 oz (200 g) pork skin from the butcher. Place the pork skin in a saucepan, add 6¼ cups (1½ liters) water and a pinch of salt, and boil for 20 minutes, until tender. Drain and cool, then use a very sharp knife to cut the pork skin into fine strips.

Pork crackers
Buy 7–10 oz (200–300g) pork skin from the butcher and cut it into long strips, about 1 in (2.5 cm) wide and 2–3 in (5–7.5 cm) long. Heat a wok and fry the pork skin strips for about 20 minutes over medium heat, then remove and let dry. Add 2¼ cups (500 ml) oil to the wok and heat. Fry the pork strips until golden brown and crispy. Remove the pork crackers and drain. Store in a sealed bag or airtight container until required (it will keep for 1 week).

Tamarind juice
To make tamarind juice (or tamarind water), soak ⅓ tamarind pulp to ⅔ water, then strain. Tamarind

concentrate is also available and is diluted with water, but the tangy flavor of the freshly soaked pulp is more intense.

Stir-frying in a wok

A specialty of Chinese cuisine, brought by immigrants and adopted by the then Siamese, this is the quickest way to cook food—first heating the wok over heat, then adding oil and heating until a haze appears. The hot oil sears the food to preserve freshness. Slicing the food into small pieces helps it to cook quickly and evenly, and of course you add the ingredients that need the longest cooking time first. Stir-fried dishes should be served immediately after cooking, which usually takes less than 5 minutes.

• Don't add water (or anything damp) to smoking oil, because it will create a high flame.

• Don't add garlic or chiles first to the hot oil. Garlic will burn, and chiles will give off an overpowering aroma that can make you cough. Either add these two to the oil with the other ingredients or first cook them over low heat before turning up the heat and adding the other ingredients.

Deep-frying

Thais love deep-fried food cooked until the outside is crispy and the inside still moist and tender. But we are becoming more health-conscious, aware of cholesterol concerns and so on, so there is less deep-frying now. Food should be dry before deep-frying and the oil heated to 300–360°F (150°–185°C)—if less, it will be soggy. Over 370°F (190°C), it will burn outside but be raw inside.

Crisp-frying

Ingredients including basil, chiles, garlic, shallots, dried shrimp, and fish are crispy-fried for some recipes for texture, flavor, and color. Cook quickly in the wok to crisp them without burning.

Dry-frying

Ingredients such as chiles, raw rice, galangal, and spices for curries are dry-fried in a wok to achieve a smoky, toasty taste. Heat the wok and add the spices, frying to aromatize, stirring to avoid burning.

Grilling

When Thais say grilling, they traditionally mean char-grilling over low heat to achieve a smoky flavor or over high heat like a barbecue. At home, you can use the broiler, oven, or barbecue, depending on the requirements of the recipe.

Steaming

I love this healthy method of cooking vegetables, and seafood and sticky rice are always steamed. The water should be boiling before you begin to steam; ingredients such as fish are steamed on a bed of cabbage on a plate. If you have extra thick plates, the fish may take longer to cook than the time specified.

Pounding

We still use a traditional stone mortar and pestle for pounding both fresh and dried spices and herbs. Clay mortars are less often used because they break easily. They have been replaced by metal mortars used with a wooden pestle.

Most ingredients should be chopped before pounding. Adding a pinch of salt will stop the juice from wetter ingredients spraying you in the eyes. The idea is to pound everything to mash it together—many recipes call for pounding to a paste, so you should continue until you have achieved that.

Chopping and slicing

In Thai recipes, food is sliced for salads and stir-fries and chopped into small pieces for curries and other dishes. The bite-size pieces are quick to cook and easy to eat—Thais use a fork and spoon to eat with rather than a knife, so basically nothing is served that needs further slicing. The preparation has all been done in the kitchen. The intricate and delicate carving of fruit and vegetables in Royal Thai Cuisine is a great skill, an art form that is the result of much practice and the subject of great competition among cooks who specialize in it, even today. The carved fruit and vegetables are part of the meal and are not just for decoration, so eat and enjoy them.

Central Thailand

Fragrant spices & coconut milk

The cuisine of the Central region is probably the best known internationally, with an emphasis on sweeter, more subtle flavors, rather than the spicier, hotter tastes of dishes from the South or from Isan.

Coconut milk and the famous red and green curry pastes are essentials for dishes such as Green Chicken Curry (see pages 32–33). Shrimp are widely used, and duck is a favorite, a result of the Chinese influence here. Some of the well-known Thai soups come from the Central region, including Jumbo Shrimp Soup with Chiles and Lime (see pages 24–25), Chicken and Coconut Soup (see pages 26–27), as well as noodle dishes such as Stir-fried Rice Noodles with Jumbo Shrimp (see pages 52–53).

Thai people eat four or five times a day, and, because food is relatively cheap, fresh, and plentiful, they tend to eat out. Most eat locally, but Thais are happy to travel if they know the food will be good, and they love to eat somewhere famous. All types of produce are readily available in the center of the country, because the network of rivers and canals creates a fertile food bowl for growing fruit, vegetables, and rice, with plentiful river fish and seafood from the coast.

At Thailand's heart is Bangkok, a dynamic, exciting city that never sleeps, where East meets West, and the Old World meets the New. All kinds of food are available here, from curries and noodles served at street stalls, to

Fourteenth-century, 62¼-feet (19-meter) high bronze Buddha in Wat Phanan Choeng, Ayuthaya.

Thai meals in family-run restaurants, to all manner of fine-dining opportunities in international, five-star hotels. Trends may stray away from traditional presentation, but Thais are very good at combining new ideas with existing concepts and love to experiment, so there's always somewhere new and fashionable to try.

The newest restaurant at the Peninsula Bangkok, The Thipt, is Thai. The latest in world food is being served in restaurants such as 87 at the Conrad Hotel on Wireless Road, while The Oriental Bangkok is a world-famous hotel that has welcomed royalty and discerning travelers for more than 120 years and has helped to put Thai food on the map with its cookery schools.

Heavily influenced by the cuisine of the Royal Palace, dishes from the Central region have traditionally been created to appeal to all the senses, with the visual aspect playing an extremely important part in presentation. Intricate carving of fruits and vegetables and the use of flowers typify the revered Palace "look." It was King Rama IV who introduced the knife and spoon to Thailand, where previously hands had been used—chopsticks have never been used in Thailand except in Chinese restaurants or when eating Chinese noodle dishes.

In Bangkok, the Sky Train is a fantastic way to speed across the city while seeing the Royal Palace and temples, such as Wat Arun. Less than 62 miles (100 kilometers) north of Bangkok is Ayuthaya, formerly the capital city. Some of its temples have been restored, and there are night markets and some floating restaurants. South of Bangkok, the Hua Hin Peninsula is a revered strip of land that is home to royal summer palaces and hotels. Eating seafood on the jetty at Hua Hin is an unforgettable experience.

Gluay khai *bananas on sale at Damnoen Saduak floating market near Bangkok.*

hot and sour fish soup with tamarind and cilantro

Tom khlong

Hot and sour are two of the basic flavors of Thai cooking, and distinctive tamarind and tangy lemon provide the sour base for this delicious soup. Dried fish, which you can find in Asian grocery stores, is traditionally used, or you can use fresh fish, as I have done here.

5 shallots, chopped and crushed

6 dried chiles, seeded and soaked in warm water

10 oz (300 g) fish filets, such as cod, or shelled and veined raw shrimp

3 cups (700 ml) Fish Stock (see page 138)

1 lemongrass stalk, finely sliced

4 slices of galangal

2 tablespoons Tamarind Juice (see pages 16–17)

¾ tablespoon fresh lime juice

3½ tablespoons fish sauce

4 whole cilantro leaves, to garnish

Preheat the oven to 325°F (160°C). Wrap the crushed shallots and dried chiles in foil to make a sealed package. Rinse and pat dry the fish filets or shrimp and put on to a baking sheet. Put both the foil package and the fish into the oven and cook for 10 minutes.

Remove both items from the oven. Cut the fish into bite-size pieces, discarding any bones.

Bring the stock to a boil, then add the lemongrass, baked shallots, baked dried chiles, galangal, and fish and simmer for 10 minutes, until the fish is done. Skim off the soup and season with the tamarind juice, lime juice, and fish sauce to obtain a sour and salty taste. Add the cilantro leaves, and serve.

Hot
Serves 4 as part of a Thai meal
Preparation and cooking time: 40 minutes

Fresh tamarind and young leaves are used to add an important "sour" taste to Thai dishes.

jumbo shrimp soup with chiles and lime

Tom yum goong

This classic soup is hot, spicy, sour, and aromatic all at the same time. For many people around the world who love Thai food, *Tom Yum Goong* soup is a measure of the quality of the chef, and many people swear by this soup to clear their heads when they have a cold!

4½ cups (1 L) Fish Stock (see page 138)

1 lemongrass stalk, sliced into rings

4 slices of galangal

4 kaffir lime leaves, torn

1½ tablespoons Roasted Chili Paste (see page 14)

4 hot chiles, or to taste

8 straw or button mushrooms, quartered

8 raw jumbo shrimp, shelled and veined

4 tablespoons fresh lime juice

4½ tablespoons fish sauce

1 tablespoon chopped cilantro

1 tablespoon finely sliced scallion

8 cilantro leaves, to garnish

Bring the stock to a boil in a large saucepan or stockpot, add the lemongrass, galangal, kaffir lime leaves, and roasted chili paste, and simmer for about 20 minutes.

Increase the heat and bring to a boil, add the chiles and mushrooms, and bring back to a boil. Add the jumbo shrimp, cook for 2 minutes, then add the lime juice, fish sauce, chopped cilantro, and scallion. Stir together briefly and serve garnished with cilantro leaves.

Hot
Serves 4 as part of a Thai meal
Preparation and cooking time: 40 minutes

Fresh jumbo shrimp this size (approx. 7 ounces/200 grams) are available year-round.

chicken and coconut soup
Tom kha gai

This dish balances the sweetness of coconut milk and the fragrance of galangal, kaffir lime leaves, and lemongrass, with the salty fish sauce and the sour taste of lime juice. The fried chiles add a smoky flavor as well as texture, color, and heat, but not so much that it overwhelms the soup.

2¼ cups (500 ml) Chicken Stock
(see page 138)

4 kaffir lime leaves, torn in half

1 lemongrass stalk, crushed

12 thin slices of galangal

10 oz (300 g) chicken breasts,
thinly sliced

2¼ cups (500 ml) Coconut Milk
(see page 16)

¾ cup (60 g) straw mushrooms
(or button or field mushrooms)

4 tablespoons fresh lime juice

4½ tablespoons fish sauce

8 small crispy-fried chiles

8 cilantro leaves, to garnish

Heat the chicken stock in a large, deep saucepan, then add the lime leaves, lemongrass, and galangal. Simmer for 10 minutes, then add the chicken and coconut milk and bring to a boil.

Add the mushrooms, lime juice, and fish sauce to the saucepan and bubble, uncovered, until the chicken is done, about 20 minutes. Add the fried chiles to the soup and serve immediately, garnished with cilantro leaves.

Medium-hot
Serves 4 as part of a Thai meal
Preparation and cooking time: 25 minutes

Monkeys are trained to collect coconuts—young or old coconuts are selected according to the trainer's call.

banana flower salad
yum hau pee

This is a wonderful Thai dish that combines the deliciously rich and creamy flavor of the banana flower with crunchy cashew nuts and the heat of roasted chiles. Banana flowers are actually the buds of the banana plant, which are soaked and shredded for use in salads. They are also available preserved from Asian grocery stores—soak in cold water for 10 minutes and rinse before using.

4½ cups (1 L) cold water

3½ oz (100 g) skinless, boneless chicken breast, sliced

3½ oz (100 g) raw jumbo shrimp, shelled and veined

1 banana flower, weighing about 7 oz (200 g)

2 tablespoons fresh lime juice

¼ cup (50 g) dried shrimp, finely chopped

1 tablespoon sliced shallots

2 tablespoons roasted cashew nuts, crushed

8 crispy-fried chiles

1 shallot, sliced and fried

Handful of cilantro leaves and 3 pieces of banana flower, to garnish

DRESSING

2½ tablespoons fish sauce

3 tablespoons fresh lime juice

½ tablespoon palm sugar

1½ tablespoons Roasted Chili Paste (see page 14)

¼ teaspoon dried, roasted chili powder

3 tablespoons Coconut Milk (see page 16)

Bring 2¼ cups (500 ml) of water to a boil in a saucepan, then add the chicken pieces, reduce to a simmer, and cook for 5 minutes. Add the shrimp and continue simmering for 3 minutes, until done. Remove the chicken and the shrimp and set aside. Discard water.

Remove and discard all the hard leaves from the banana flower, then thinly slice the white inside part diagonally. Mix the lime juice with 2¼ cups (500 ml) of cold water and soak the banana flower slices for 5 minutes to prevent discoloration.

Make the dressing. In a bowl, combine the fish sauce, lime juice, palm sugar, chili paste, chili powder, and coconut milk. Mix them together well until the palm sugar has completely dissolved.

Gently squeeze the water from the banana flower and then combine it with the dressing, the chicken and shrimp, dried shrimp, tablespoon of sliced shallots, and cashew nuts. Mix well, then serve sprinkled with the crispy-fried chiles and fried shallots, and garnish with cilantro leaves and banana flower pieces.

Medium-hot
Serves 4 as part of a Thai meal
Preparation and cooking time: 1 hour

jungle chicken curry
gaeng pa gai

This aromatic and highly spiced curry is one of the five hottest dishes in Thailand, traditionally made with anything and everything available in the jungle! My grandfather loved to eat this once a week, believing that it was good for the digestion and that it kept influenza away—a tradition he continued until his death at the ripe old age of 95.

1 tablespoon Red Curry Paste
  (see page 15)
1 tablespoon chopped garlic
1 tablespoon chopped red chile
1 tablespoon vegetable oil
1 tablespoon lesser ginger
3 stalks green peppercorns,
  fresh or preserved
7 oz (200 g) chicken breast
  filets, sliced
1½ cups (350 ml) Chicken Stock
  (see page 138)
4 kaffir lime leaves
½ cup (50 g) sliced bamboo
  shoots
4 pieces of baby corn (other
  vegetables can be added, too,
  such as broccoli and carrots)
½ cup (30 g) wood or cloud ear
  mushrooms (or use field
  mushrooms)
Handful of holy basil
3 teaspoons fish sauce
1 teaspoon palm sugar

Using a mortar and pestle, pound the red curry paste together with the garlic and chile until fine. Heat a heavy-bottomed saucepan, add the oil and the pounded paste, and fry, stirring together until the paste turns light brown.

Add the lesser ginger and peppercorns and stir-fry for 2 minutes, until fragrant, then add the chicken and cook for a further 2 minutes. Now, pour in the stock, add the kaffir lime leaves, and bring to a boil. Add the bamboo shoots, baby corn (and any other vegetables), mushrooms, holy basil, fish sauce, and palm sugar. Cook for a further 5 minutes.

Very hot
Serves 4 as part of a Thai meal
Preparation and cooking time: 20 minutes

Fresh krachai *(lesser ginger) on sale at a gas station's stall.*

green chicken curry
gaeng khiao wan gai

A favorite dish in Thai restaurants around the world, *gaeng khiao wan gai* means "green sweet curry," the sweetness deriving from the coconut milk and the palm sugar. It is also deliciously hot and aromatic, thanks to the green curry paste, peppercorns, kaffir lime leaves, and sweet basil, and salty through the shrimp paste and fish sauce.

Scant 1 cup (200 ml) coconut cream, plus 1 tablespoon to garnish

1 tablespoon Green Curry Paste (see page 15)

4 kaffir lime leaves, torn

10 oz (300 g) chicken breast filets, sliced

4 tablespoons fish sauce

2 teaspoons palm sugar

1¾ cups (400 ml) Coconut Milk (see page 16)

3 Thai eggplants, quartered (or green beans or fresh green peas)

2 long red chiles, sliced diagonally

Handful of Thai sweet basil (reserve a few leaves to garnish)

Heat the coconut cream in a medium saucepan over low heat. Add the green curry paste and stir, cooking for about 4–5 minutes until the green curry paste oil separates and rises to the surface.

Add the kaffir lime leaves and the chicken slices to the saucepan. Cook, stirring, for 2 minutes, then add the fish sauce, palm sugar, coconut milk, and the Thai eggplants. Boil (uncovered) for a further 7 minutes until the chicken is done, stirring often to prevent sticking and burning.

Add the sliced chiles and basil, stirring together for about 1 minute. Serve the curry in a bowl, garnished with 1 tablespoon of coconut cream and the reserved basil leaves.

Hot
Serves 4 as part of a Thai meal
Preparation and cooking time: 30 minutes

Traditional home beside a klong (canal) in Central Thailand.

red duck curry
with pineapple

gaeng ped pet yang kai khem

The use of pineapple in this recipe is an example of the Thai tradition of balancing flavors, adding sweetness to offset the richness of the duck. Very old recipes include salty eggs, which are made by preserving fresh, uncooked duck eggs in a brine solution for three weeks or longer. Salty eggs are available from Asian stores, if you wish to include one; stir in over the heat just before serving.

13½ oz (400 g) roasted duck
  meat
½ cup (100 ml) coconut cream
2 tablespoons Red Curry Paste
  (see page 15)
1¾ cups (400 ml) Coconut Milk
  (see page 16)
5 kaffir lime leaves, finely sliced
3½ tablespoons fish sauce
4 teaspoons palm sugar
8 cherry tomatoes
3 long red chiles, sliced
3½ oz (100 g) fresh pineapple,
  cut into chunks
Handful of Thai sweet basil
Rice, to serve

Slice the cooked duck into roughly 1-in (about 3-cm) long pieces. Heat the coconut cream in a saucepan over medium heat, add the red curry paste, and stir for about 7–10 minutes, until the curry paste oil separates and rises to the surface. Stir well. Reserve 1 teaspoon of the coconut milk for garnish and slowly add the remainder to the saucepan.

Add the kaffir lime leaves and stir over low heat for about 5 minutes, then add the fish sauce and the palm sugar and cook until the oil again rises to the surface. Now, add the duck pieces, cherry tomatoes, chiles, and pineapple chunks. Reserve two or three Thai basil leaves for garnish and add the remainder to the saucepan. Boil together for 3 minutes, then garnish with the reserved coconut milk and basil leaves, and serve with plain rice.

Medium-hot
Serves 4 as part of a Thai meal
Preparation and cooking time: 30 minutes

stir-fried lamb with holy basil

lamb pad krapao

Holy basil is a classic ingredient in Thai stir-fry dishes made with shrimp, pork, and, here, lamb. Thais like nothing better than to serve the *pad krapao* with fried egg, rice, and fish sauce with slices of hot chile.

2 tablespoons vegetable oil

1 tablespoon finely chopped garlic

1 teaspoon chopped small red chiles

Handful of holy basil

10 oz (300 g) lamb filets, sliced into 3-in (7-cm) pieces

½ onion, finely sliced

1 tablespoon soy sauce

1 tablespoon fish sauce

1 tablespoon oyster sauce

1 teaspoon superfine sugar

2 long red chiles, sliced

2 scallions, cut into 2-in (5-cm) pieces

Handful of crispy-fried Thai sweet basil

Heat the oil in a wok until it smokes, then add the garlic, chopped chiles, and holy basil. Quickly stir-fry for 10–15 seconds, until fragrant.

Add the lamb pieces and stir-fry until sealed, then add the onion, soy sauce, fish sauce, oyster sauce, and sugar. Cook, stirring constantly, until the meat is medium rare—sealed on the outside, but still pink and juicy inside.

Add the sliced red chiles and scallions to the wok, stir to mix, and serve immediately, garnished with the crispy-fried Thai sweet basil.

Hot
Serves 4 as part of a Thai meal
Preparation and cooking time: 20 minutes

Modern equipment plus traditional people power speed the rice harvest.

panang beef
gaeng panang nue

This recipe is usually made with beef, but regular customers of the Arun Thai restaurant in Sydney have also grown to love our chicken version. You can also use shrimp or other seafood, or pork. This very traditional Thai curry is thicker than most because of the mung beans in the Panang curry paste, which help to create the deliciously thick sauce.

½ cup (100 ml) coconut cream
1 tablespoon Panang Curry
  Paste (see page 15)
14 oz (400 g) beef sirloin, sliced
1½ cups (350 ml) Coconut Milk
  (see page 16)
3 kaffir lime leaves
3 tablespoons fish sauce
1 teaspoon palm sugar
1 small red chile, sliced
Handful of Thai sweet basil

Heat the coconut cream in a heavy-bottomed saucepan over medium heat, add the curry paste, and stir until the paste oil separates and rises to the surface.

Stir in the beef, mixing well with the coconut cream mixture. Reserve 1 tablespoon of the coconut milk for garnish and add the remainder to the saucepan, together with two of the kaffir lime leaves, roughly torn. Simmer for 10 minutes, stirring often, then blend in the fish sauce and palm sugar, and simmer for a further 5 minutes until the beef is done and the curry has thickened.

Serve garnished with the reserved tablespoon of coconut milk, sliced chile, the remaining kaffir lime leaf, finely sliced, and a handful of Thai sweet basil leaves.

Medium-hot
Serves 4 as part of a Thai meal
Preparation and cooking time: 30 minutes

Detail from the beautiful Wat Arun in Bangkok.

steamed salmon in young coconut

hor mok pla

Traditional *hor mok* is a steamed red curry made with fish, chicken, or seafood and wrapped in a banana leaf, but this dish can also be steamed in a whole young coconut for a toasty, aromatic flavor and a delicious taste. You need a deep steamer large enough to accommodate the coconut. If you can't find a young coconut, you can also steam the mixture in foil, which will take about 25 minutes.

1 fresh green coconut

2½ oz (80 g) white fish filets, such as sole or whiting, sliced

1 tablespoon Red Curry Paste (see page 15)

1 cup (250 ml) coconut cream

1 egg, beaten

1 tablespoon lesser ginger

3 kaffir lime leaves, finely sliced

1½ tablespoons fish sauce

1½ teaspoons superfine sugar

3½ oz (100 g) salmon filets, sliced

½ teaspoon ground white pepper

12 Thai sweet basil leaves

1½ oz (50 g) Chinese cabbage, steamed

Coconut Milk (see page 16) and 2 sliced red chiles, to serve

Partially slice the top off the coconut, leaving a hinge attached to form a lid. Drain off the coconut juice and leave the coconut upside down to drain, then wipe it dry inside.

In a blender, combine the white fish and red curry paste and blend until smooth, about 5 minutes. Pour the coconut cream into a large mixing bowl, add the blended fish, egg, lesser ginger, two of the sliced kaffir lime leaves, fish sauce, sugar, salmon filets, and white pepper, and stir gently together in one direction only, in order to combine the ingredients without breaking them up. The mixture should then stick together.

Place the Thai sweet basil leaves and steamed Chinese cabbage at the bottom of the coconut, then top with the fish mixture. Close the lid of the coconut and place upright in a steamer to steam for 40 minutes. Alternatively, steam in a foil package for 25 minutes.

Serve garnished with the coconut milk, sliced chiles, and the remaining sliced kaffir lime leaf.

Medium-hot
Serves 4 as part of a Thai meal
Preparation and cooking time: 1 hour 25 minutes

steamed fish with lime juice and chiles

pla neung manao

The coastline, rivers, canals, and even the rice paddy fields of Thailand teem with fish, and many Thai people simply catch or net their own when it is time for the next meal. Select the freshest fish for this recipe. The cabbage leaves prevent the fish from sticking while it cooks.

1 lb 5 oz (600 g) firm white fish filets, such as cod or haddock

Chinese cabbage or white cabbage leaves

Handful of Thai sweet basil leaves

2 tablespoons sliced lemongrass

2 teaspoons finely chopped cilantro and 2 whole cilantro leaves, to garnish

3 slices of lime (or lemon), to garnish

Rice and stir-fried vegetables, to serve

SAUCE
5 hot red chiles
3 garlic cloves
2 tablespoons fish sauce
3 tablespoons fresh lime juice
1 teaspoon superfine sugar

Rinse the fish filets, pat them dry and, using a sharp knife, carefully score about three times on each side.

Line a medium-size plate with the cabbage leaves, sprinkle over the Thai sweet basil leaves and sliced lemongrass, and lay the fish filets on top. Place the plate in a steamer, cover, and steam over boiling water for 15 minutes.

To make the sauce, chop the chiles and garlic cloves and combine in a bowl with the fish sauce, lime juice, and sugar, mixing well until the sugar dissolves.

When the fish is done, remove the plate from the steamer, drain off the juices, and transfer to a serving dish. Spoon over the sauce and sprinkle with the finely chopped cilantro. Garnish with the whole cilantro leaves and lime slices and serve with plain rice and some colorful stir-fried vegetables.

Very hot
Serves 4 as part of a Thai meal
Preparation and cooking time: 20 minutes

fried salmon with chu chee curry sauce

chu chee pla salmon

Chu chee is a traditional curry sauce for seafood, such as shrimp and scallops. Here, I have combined it with salmon, because the strong flavor, color, and texture of the fish go particularly well with this rich red curry sauce.

CHU CHEE SAUCE
½ cup (100 ml) coconut cream
½ tablespoon Red Curry Paste (see page 15)
½ tablespoon Panang Curry Paste (see page 15)
Scant 1 cup (200 ml) Coconut Milk (see page 16)
2 tablespoons fish sauce
2 teaspoons palm sugar
½ cup (100 ml) vegetable oil

13½ oz (400 g) salmon filets
5 Thai sweet basil leaves
1 kaffir lime leaf, finely sliced
1 hot red chile, finely sliced

First, make the sauce. Gently heat the coconut cream in a medium saucepan and add the curry pastes. Cook, stirring, for about 5 minutes, until the curry paste oil separates and rises to the surface. Add the coconut milk, fish sauce, and palm sugar and simmer for 7 minutes, stirring often. Set aside and keep warm.

Heat the oil in a skillet and fry the salmon until golden brown. Remove the salmon and add to the warm *Chu Chee sauce*, shaking gently to coat the salmon. Transfer the salmon and sauce to a serving dish and garnish with basil leaves, kaffir lime leaves, and sliced chile.

Medium-hot
Serves 4 as part of a Thai meal
Preparation and cooking time: 30 minutes

Buying snacks from a street stall to take home to the children.

stir-fried clams with chile and basil

hoi lai pad horapha

Stir-fried shellfish is quick and easy to cook. This is a delicious way to serve clams or mussels, with hot chile, soy sauce, and basil. The important thing is to ensure that the wok is hot before you begin to add the ingredients.

13½ oz (500 g) fresh clams (or mussels), in the shell
2 tablespoons vegetable oil
1 small red chile, finely chopped
1 teaspoon finely chopped garlic
1 tablespoon Roasted Chili Paste (see page 14)
¾ tablespoon fish sauce
¾ tablespoon oyster sauce
1 teaspoon superfine sugar
1 tablespoon Fish Stock (see page 138)
Handful of Thai sweet basil leaves

Rinse the clams thoroughly and drain. Discard any that have not closed.

Heat the oil in a wok or skillet and add the chile and garlic. Stir-fry quickly until the garlic is golden brown—less than 1 minute. Add the clams and stir them until they open. Discard any that do not open. Add the roasted chili paste, fish sauce, oyster sauce, and sugar and stir, then pour in the fish stock. Cover and cook for 3 minutes. Add the basil, stir briefly, and serve immediately.

Medium-hot
Serves 4 as part of a Thai meal
Preparation and cooking time: 25 minutes

Mobile juice sellers quench the thirst of Bangkok's busy workers.

stir-fried scampi with krachai and peppercorns

pad char scampi

This deliciously spicy dish is made without coconut milk. For the very best results, the *Pad Char* paste should be freshly made—there are quite a few ingredients, but it doesn't take long to combine them into an exquisitely fragrant paste! Fresh lesser ginger (*krachai*) is best, but not always widely available, so find the pickled variety in jars and rinse well in cold water before using.

PAD CHAR PASTE

8–10 slices red chile

3 shallots, peeled and sliced

3 garlic cloves, peeled and chopped

1 lemongrass stalk, finely chopped

1 tablespoon finely chopped galangal

1 tablespoon chopped lesser ginger

2 kaffir lime leaves

4 stalks of green peppercorns, fresh or preserved

3 tablespoons vegetable oil

12 raw scampi (or jumbo shrimp), shelled, veined, and halved

3 tablespoons Chicken Stock (see page 138)

1½ tablespoons fish sauce

1 tablespoon oyster sauce

1 tablespoon soy sauce

2 teaspoons superfine sugar

¾ cup (100 g) green beans

Handful of Thai sweet basil leaves

Handful of holy basil leaves

To make the paste, pound the chile and shallots using a mortar and pestle until fine, then transfer to a hot, dry wok with the garlic, lemongrass, galangal, lesser ginger, kaffir lime leaves, and green peppercorns. Fry over gentle heat for about 1 minute, until everything is well mixed and fragrant. You will know the paste is ready the moment you begin to smell the wonderful aroma. Remove the wok from the heat, transfer the paste to a bowl, and set aside.

Add the oil to the wok and heat until it smokes. Add the *Pad Char* paste, stirring for 2 minutes, then add the scampi. Stir well and add the chicken stock, fish sauce, oyster sauce, soy sauce, sugar, and green beans. Cover with a lid and bubble for 1 minute, then add the basil leaves, toss through, and serve immediately.

Hot
Serves 4 as part of a Thai meal
Preparation and cooking time: 30 minutes

Fishing boats at Rayong catch anchovies—the main ingredient for making fish sauce— each day.

stir-fried crab with yellow curry sauce

pu pad pong khari

This combines Chinese stir-fry and Indian curry influences with two very important Thai ingredients—chiles and garlic. Preparing crab can be rather fiddly, but it is well worth the effort. Shelled raw shrimp can be used instead of the crab, if preferred.

1 fresh uncooked crab,
  weighing about 1 lb 2 oz
  (500 g)
4 red chiles
2 garlic cloves, peeled
2 tablespoons vegetable oil
½ cup (100 ml) milk
1 egg
1 tablespoon soy sauce
1 tablespoon oyster sauce
2 teaspoons superfine sugar
1 teaspoon ground white
  pepper
2 teaspoons medium to hot
  curry powder
⅓ cup (80 g) sliced onion
⅓ cup (80 g) chopped scallions

Wash the crab, remove the shell and claw, then chop the crab into six pieces using a cleaver. Using the back of the cleaver, lightly crack the claws to make them easy to open.

Pound two of the chiles and garlic together using a mortar and pestle. Heat the oil in a wok, add the pounded chiles and garlic, and stir for about 1 minute. Slice the remaining chiles and add to the wok. Add the crab and stir for about 8 minutes, until it turns pink.

Beat the milk and egg together in a bowl and add to the crab, cooking for 2–3 minutes, then add the soy sauce, oyster sauce, sugar, pepper, and curry powder, stirring well to mix. Add the sliced onion and chopped scallions. Cover with a lid and cook for about 2 minutes until the sauce thickens, then check that the crab is done, using the tip of a knife to part the flesh of the largest chunks. Cooked crabmeat is white. Transfer to a serving plate, arrange, and serve.

Medium-hot
Serves 4 as part of a Thai meal
Preparation and cooking time: 30 minutes

Crabs from Southern Thailand are available year-round and are favorites in the Central and Northern regions of the country.

stir-fried rice noodles with jumbo shrimp

pad thai goong

Noodles and stir-frying were introduced to Thailand by Chinese immigrants, and both fitted easily into Thai cooking principles because they were quick to prepare and very tasty. *Pad thai* (stir-fried Thai noodles) are widely available from street stalls all over Thailand and are one of the most famous of all Thai dishes. They are particularly delicious with duck eggs.

7 oz (200 g) medium rice stick noodles

1½ tablespoons vegetable oil

2 teaspoons dried shrimp

8 raw jumbo shrimp, shelled and veined

2 eggs (use duck eggs if you like)

3 tablespoons cubed firm tofu (bean curd)

1 tablespoon pickled radish (optional)

5 teaspoons superfine sugar

2 tablespoons fish sauce

3 tablespoons Tamarind Juice (see pages 16–17)

2 teaspoons chili powder, or to taste

1 cup (80 g) bean sprouts

10 Chinese chives, chopped into 3-in (7.5-cm) lengths

2 tablespoons ground roasted peanuts

1 lime, quartered

Banana blossom

Soak the rice noodles in warm water for 15 minutes, then remove and drain.

Heat the oil in a wok, add the dried shrimp, and cook until golden brown. Add the jumbo shrimp and stir until cooked, about 2 minutes. Then add the eggs, tofu, pickled radish, rice noodles, sugar, fish sauce, tamarind juice, 1 teaspoon of chili powder, and half the bean sprouts and stir well until the noodles are cooked.

Add half the chives and stir. Serve garnished with the remaining bean sprouts and chives, ground roasted peanuts, lime wedges, and a banana blossom, if possible. Offer the second teaspoon of chili powder in a little pile, so that it can be stirred in to taste.

Spicy
Serves 4 as part of a Thai meal
Preparation and cooking time: 25 minutes

roasted tofu with chile, cilantro, and mushrooms

Taohu ob

Good for a healthy diet, tofu (bean curd) has been eaten in northern Asia for many thousands of years. Following its introduction, it soon became a very popular ingredient in Thai cuisine. The silken tofu used in this recipe is good for roasting and for soups—here, it is placed over the other ingredients and the saucepan is shaken, not stirred, to avoid breaking up the tofu.

1 tablespoon vegetable oil

1-inch (2.5-cm) piece gingerroot, sliced into fine strips

1 small red chile, crushed

2 garlic cloves, crushed

2 cilantro roots, crushed

½ teaspoon ground white pepper

1½ tablespoons oyster sauce

1½ tablespoons soy sauce

1 teaspoon superfine sugar

1 lb 2 oz (500 g) silken tofu (bean curd)

1 cup (250 ml) Vegetable Stock (see page 138)

3 scallions, cut into 3-in (7-cm) pieces

¾ cup (50 g) brown, oyster, shiitake, or *hed kon* (wild) mushrooms, finely sliced

Whole cilantro leaves and a few slices of chile, to garnish

Heat the oil in a deep saucepan with the ginger, chile, garlic, cilantro, pepper, oyster sauce, soy sauce, and sugar and place the tofu on top. Pour in the vegetable stock, cover with a lid, and cook for about 7 minutes to reduce the liquid, occasionally shaking the saucepan to prevent sticking.

Remove the lid, add the scallions and mushrooms, and cook, covered, for a further 2 minutes. Garnish with cilantro leaves and chile slices and serve immediately.

Medium-hot
Serves 4 as part of a Thai meal
Preparation and cooking time: 25 minutes

A great delicacy, hed kon *mushrooms grow on old timbers when the rains come.*

crispy fish salad with green mango

yum pla duk foo

In Thailand, this would be made with catfish, a tasty river fish that is popular throughout Asia because its texture is perfect for frying until crisp. To make this recipe, choose a fine-textured rather than a flaky fish to make it easier to fry. Green apple can be substituted for green mango. Serve the salad at room temperature, or cold.

7 oz (200 g) catfish or other white fish filets

2¼ cups (500 ml) vegetable oil

1 tablespoon (10 g) all-purpose flour

½ cup (100 g) grated green mango or green apple

3 tablespoons cashew nuts

Cilantro leaves, to garnish

SAUCE

2½ tablespoons fish sauce

2 tablespoons fresh lime juice

2 teaspoons palm sugar

2 shallots, peeled and sliced

1 red chile, sliced

Steam the fish fillets in a steamer for about 10 minutes. Remove from the heat, pat dry with paper towels, and use a fork to break the filets into pieces. Heat the oil in a medium, heavy-bottomed skillet, deep enough for the oil to cover the fish.

Coat the fish pieces in the flour and deep-fry until golden brown. Remove the fish from the oil and drain on paper towels. Transfer the fish pieces to a serving plate and top with grated green mango.

To make the sauce, put the fish sauce, lime juice, and palm sugar in a bowl and stir until the sugar has dissolved, then add the shallots and chile. Mix well and pour over the fish and mango salad. Scatter over the cashew nuts and cilantro leaves and serve.

Medium-hot
Serves 4 as part of a Thai meal
Preparation and cooking time: 30 minutes

Green mangoes piled high in the markets.

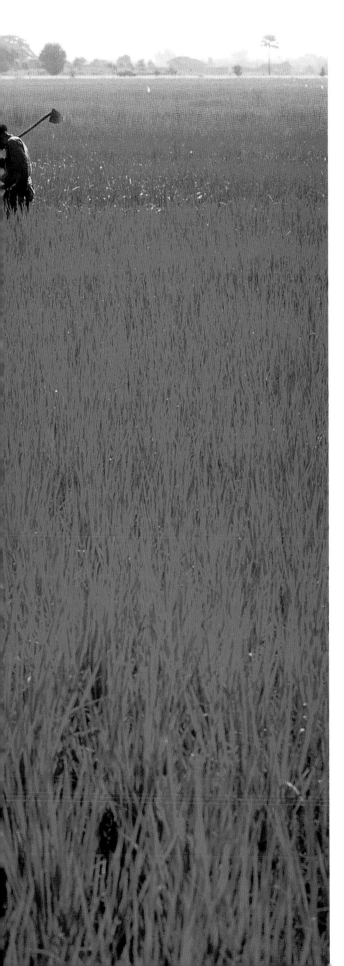

Isan—the Northeast

Fresh herbs & hot chiles

I was brought up beside the Mekong River and spent a great deal of time both on it and in it. I am Thai, although my birthplace was Savannakhet on the Laos side, but we didn't think of the two sides as different countries at all, because the water was like a highway to us. After school, my friends and I would swim the 1 mile (1½ kilometers) across this famous river to play with children on the Mukdahan (Thai) side. When we weren't swimming it, we were crisscrossing it at great speed in the longtail water taxis.

Sharing the long Mekong River, Isan has more similarities with Laos than with the other regions of Thailand. In the Northeast of the region, people speak Lao and are referred to as Lao by other Thais. Further south, Khmer is spoken in the areas bordering Cambodia. All through Isan, you can see the influences in the shared architecture of the temples as well as in the food.

Isan food is very fresh and uncomplicated, known for its robust flavors. The northeast is not a fertile region, because the hot, dry season is followed by rains that cause flooding, so the friendly people here are used to tough conditions and to making do with whatever food is available. Despite this, feasts are much enjoyed here, with blessings from the monks and the elders to celebrate weddings and special occasions.

Sticky rice is a Thai staple, used a bit like bread, and the Isan tradition is to eat with the hands, dipping balls of sticky rice into sauces and curry dishes. Our salads (*larb*)

Farmer working in the rice fields after the welcome rainy season in Isan.

are served Laotian-style, but ingredients such as duck and fish are chopped rather than minced, as they are in Laos, and mixed with fresh mint, scallions, chiles, lime juice, and ground roasted rice.

I was lucky to be brought up so close to the river, where plenty of fish was available—Thais love fresh fish of any description. Isan is infamous for *pla ra*, an extremely strong-smelling fermented fish, which is served with sticky rice. Bottled fish sauce is also widely used.

The region is generally poor, but what dishes lack in the refinement of the coconut milk and spices of the South, they make up for in the heat of chiles and the fresh tastes of mint, scallion, cilantro, lime, and lemon basil. Special Isan dishes include Crying Tiger (see pages 78–79), grilled beef served with a fresh, hot spicy sauce, spicy salads, Waterfall Beef Salad (see pages 68–69), Isan Mushroom Salad (see pages 70–71), and the famous spicy Papaya Salad (see pages 66–67), which is loved throughout Thailand. All the Isan dishes go perfectly with sticky rice.

Recently on a visit to Isan, I noticed that times have really changed—the airport is bigger, and the road from the Southern and Central region is much faster now. For cooking, the variety of ingredients is much wider, but the basic ingredients for Isan cooking are still the same. A dish I was thrilled to eat again for the first time in many years was *yum hed kon*, a very rare mushroom with a sweet, exotic taste found only during the rainy season growing on the nest of the white ant. I was enjoying this in a restaurant in Nong Khai when I also saw a street vendor pass by with a basket full of fresh lotus seeds. I had to run after her and buy some. With all the delicacy of rose petals, their flavor is exquisite.

The Mekong River divides Thailand and Laos, but the culture as well as the dialect and food is very similar on both sides of the river.

isan sour fish soup
gaeng som pla isan

Isan soups are clear and clean-tasting, very different to the chili paste-based *tom yum* soups of the Central region. Any white fish, such as cod or angler fish, is suitable for this soup. The stock for the soup must be boiling before you add the fish, or the fishy taste will be overpowering. If you prefer less heat, use only one or two chiles.

8 slices galangal

2–4 hot chiles, to taste

4 cloves garlic, chopped

2 shallots, sliced

1 lemongrass stalk, cut into
  2-in (5-cm) pieces

4½ cups (1 L) Fish Stock (see
  page 138)

4 kaffir lime leaves, torn

1 lb 2 oz (500 g) white fish
  filets, sliced into 2-in (5-cm)
  pieces

8 cherry tomatoes

4 tablespoons Tamarind Juice
  (see pages 16–17)

3½ tablespoons fish sauce

1 tablespoon fresh lime juice

1 cup (100 g) straw mushrooms

1 tablespoon finely chopped
  cilantro

1 scallion, cut into 2-in (5-cm)
  pieces

2 sprigs of dill

Using a mortar and pestle, pound the galangal, chiles, garlic, shallots, and lemongrass until fine.

Heat 1¼ cup (300 ml) of the fish stock in a saucepan, then add the pounded ingredients and the torn kaffir lime leaves. Bring to a boil, then reduce the heat and simmer for 10 minutes to aromatize.

Add the remaining fish stock and bring to a boil once more, then add the fish filets. Cook for about 8 minutes, until the fish is done. Add the cherry tomatoes, season with the tamarind juice, fish sauce, and lime juice, then drop in the mushrooms and continue to cook for about 2 minutes. Serve the soup hot, sprinkled with cilantro and chopped scallion. Garnish with dill sprigs.

Hot
Serves 4 as part of a Thai meal
Preparation and cooking time: 30 minutes

Mekong ferry boats carry passengers and goods of all kinds between towns and villages in Laos and Thailand.

isan duck salad
larb pet isan

One of the great Thai classics, originally from the eastern part of Thailand, this dish combines meat and herbs with lime juice for an explosion of irresistible, spicy, fresh tastes. This goes well with sticky rice and is perfectly balanced by the coolness of the lettuce and cucumber.

10 oz (300 g) fresh duck breasts
  (or use ready-roasted duck)
4 slices galangal
4 tablespoons fresh lime juice
2 teaspoons superfine sugar
3 tablespoons fish sauce
1 shallot, finely sliced
½ teaspoon chili powder
Handful of mint leaves
1 tablespoon ground rice
1 scallion, chopped
2 lemongrass stalks, finely sliced
1 tablespoon chopped cilantro
Lettuce leaves, cucumber slices,
  green beans, crispy-fried
  chiles, and whole, fresh
  chiles, to serve

If you are using fresh duck, broil the breasts for about 7 minutes each side. Wrap the galangal in foil and broil for 5 minutes. When this is done, chop the duck and the galangal into fine slices.

Mix the lime juice, sugar, and fish sauce in a bowl until the sugar dissolves, then add the duck and galangal mixture, shallot, chili powder, mint, ground rice, scallion, lemongrass, and cilantro and mix well, so all the flavors are combined. Serve with lettuce, cucumber slices, green beans, crispy-fried chiles, and fresh chiles on the side.

Hot
Serves 4 as part of a Thai meal
Preparation and cooking time: 40 minutes

Hungry Isan people wait for freshly cooked food at house-front stalls.

papaya salad with grilled chicken

som tum gai yang

Huge quantities of this are consumed every day in Thailand, so it is very much a national dish. Tomato and papaya are used all over the country, but the Thai people in the Northeast traditionally use fermented fish and fermented crabs in addition to fish sauce.

1 fresh chicken, weighing
  2 lb 12 oz (1.2 kg)

MARINADE

2 garlic cloves

2 cilantro roots

2 teaspoons superfine sugar

2 tablespoons light soy sauce

½ teaspoon salt

PAPAYA SALAD

3 garlic cloves

3 bird's eye chiles

¼ cup (30 g) roasted peanuts

2 tablespoons (30 g) dried
  shrimp

8 cherry tomatoes

3 tablespoons fish sauce

2 teaspoons palm sugar

4½ tablespoons fresh lime juice

1½ cups (250 g) sliced green
  papaya

4 lettuce leaves

4 green beans, halved

Cut the chicken in half lengthwise using poultry scissors, or ask your butcher to do this for you.

To make the marinade, put the garlic and cilantro in a large bowl and pound together, then add the sugar, soy sauce, and salt. Put the spatchcocked chicken on a plate and rub the mixture all over it, inside and out, then cover with plastic wrap and leave in the refrigerator overnight.

When you are ready to eat, grill or broil the chicken for 15–20 minutes over medium heat, then slice the meat off the bone.

Make the papaya salad. Using a mortar and pestle, pound the garlic, chiles, peanuts, and dried shrimp to a fine paste. Mix the paste with the cherry tomatoes, fish sauce, palm sugar, and lime juice. Mix well, then add the green beans and papaya. Stir to mix without breaking up the papaya, then serve with the hot chicken and lettuce leaves on the side.

Hot
Serves 4 as part of a Thai meal
Preparation and cooking time: Overnight for marinating the chicken, 30 minutes for salad

waterfall beef salad
nue yang nam tok

In Northeastern Thailand, beef is traditionally cooked over charcoal, and it is the juices running off it that give this dish its name, which literally means "waterfall beef." The tender beef strips are spiked with spicy, pungent flavors and served with a cooling salad of cucumber, lettuce, mint, and a little fresh chile. The Thai way to eat this is with your hands, gathering up all the ingredients so you have a taste of everything in each bite.

10½ oz (300 g) piece sirloin steak
3 tablespoons fish sauce
3½ tablespoons fresh lime juice
1 teaspoon palm sugar
1 tablespoon finely chopped
  cilantro
2 scallions, finely sliced
2 shallots, finely sliced
Handful of mint leaves
2 teaspoons ground rice
½ teaspoon chili powder

SALAD
To taste, including lettuce
  leaves, sliced cucumber, sliced
  scallions, cilantro
  leaves, mint leaves, whole
  fresh chiles, to taste

Grill or broil the steak, ideally to medium-rare, and slice carefully into thin strips.

Mix the fish sauce, lime juice, and palm sugar together in a bowl until the sugar has dissolved, then add the beef strips. Add the cilantro, scallions, shallots, mint leaves, ground rice, and chili powder and mix well.

To serve, assemble the salad on a plate and serve with the sliced beef.

Hot
Serves 4 as part of a Thai meal
Preparation and cooking time: 25 minutes

Sausages and meatballs on sale at the Isan markets.

isan mushroom salad

soop hed isan

In the Isan dialect, *soop* actually means salad, and this recipe, with a Lao influence, is a bowl of moist seasoned mushrooms to eat with sticky rice. In Thailand, the shallots, chiles, and garlic would be wrapped in banana leaves and cooked over a fire, but broiling will help to achieve a degree of the smoky flavor.

2¼ cups (200 g) oyster
  mushrooms
  (or any white mushrooms)
1 shallot, unpeeled
1 or 2 small red chiles, to taste
2 garlic cloves, unpeeled
2 tablespoons fish sauce
2 tablespoons fresh lime juice
1 tablespoon superfine sugar
1 scallion, finely chopped
1 tablespoon finely chopped
  cilantro
Lettuce, cucumber, and Thai
  eggplants, to serve

Broil the mushrooms, shallot, chiles, and garlic (all unpeeled) for about 6 minutes, until they change color. Remove and leave to cool. When cool enough to handle, peel off the skin from the shallot and garlic, then, using a mortar and pestle, pound the flesh of the shallot, chiles, and garlic until finely ground.

Mix the fish sauce, lime juice, and sugar in a serving bowl until the sugar dissolves, then add the pounded shallot, chiles, and garlic. Tear the mushrooms into strips and add them to the mixture together with the chopped scallion and cilantro. Stir and serve with lettuce, cucumber, and Thai eggplants. This dish goes well with crispy-fried fish (shown opposite) and grilled chicken or pork.

Hot
Serves 4 as part of a Thai meal
Preparation and cooking time: 20 minutes

Oyster mushrooms are widely used in Thai cooking and are available all over the world.

vegetable curry with venison

orm nue kuang

Orm means to simmer ingredients together in stock like a stew. The small native jungle deer from the Thai rainforests are nearly extinct, so today, as in many other countries, farmed venison is used.

1 red chile, or to taste
1 lemongrass stalk, finely chopped
1 shallot, sliced
5 slices galangal
4½ cups (1 L) Chicken Stock (see page 138)
14 oz (400 g) loin of venison, cut into thick strips or chunks
¾ cup (100 g) chopped zucchini
¾ cup (100 g) green beans, cut into 1-in (2.5-cm) slices
½ cup (50g) butternut squash, peeled and sliced into bite-size pieces
2 Thai eggplants, quartered
4 tablespoons fish sauce
1 tablespoon superfine sugar
2 scallions, sliced into 1-in (2.5-cm) pieces
Handful of Thai sweet basil
Sprigs of dill, to garnish

Using a mortar and pestle, pound the chile, lemongrass, shallot, and galangal until fine.

Heat 1 cup (250 ml) of the chicken stock in a medium saucepan, add the pounded ingredients, and cook until you can smell the fresh, tangy aroma. Now, add the venison and the remaining chicken stock, cover, and simmer for about 1 hour, until the venison is tender.

Add all the vegetables (except the scallions) to the saucepan and cook until they are soft, then season with the fish sauce, sugar, scallions, and basil. Cook for a further 2 minutes, then serve with plain rice. Garnish with sprigs of dill.

Medium-hot
Serves 4 as part of a Thai meal
Preparation and cooking time: 2 hours

Fresh produce, like these long beans, is available in the morning markets every day.

steamed chicken in banana leaves

hor mok gai

People from my region don't use much coconut milk for cooking, opting instead for ingredients such as basil, galangal, chiles, and shallots, pounded together to form a paste that can be used as a marinade for chicken, fish, frogs' legs, vegetables, or whatever is available on the day. As well as enclosing the chicken for cooking, the banana leaves add flavor. If you cannot find them, use foil instead to wrap the chicken for steaming. Banana flowers preserved in salt and water are exported internationally from Thailand, and can be found in specialty shops. Soak them for 10 minutes, then rinse to remove the salty taste.

1 lemongrass stalk, finely sliced

2 teaspoons galangal, finely chopped

2 shallots, finely sliced

5 red chiles, sliced

½ teaspoon salt

14 oz (400 g) skinless, boneless chicken breast, sliced into chunks

2 tablespoons fish sauce

1 teaspoon superfine sugar

½ banana flower, soaked in water with 2 tablespoons fresh lime juice added to prevent discoloration

4 banana leaf pieces, cut into 6 x 6-in (15 x 15-cm) pieces

Handful of Thai basil leaves

Sliced chile and 1 teaspoon Coconut Milk (see page 16), to garnish

Using a mortar and pestle, pound the sliced lemongrass, galangal, shallots, chiles, and salt.

Transfer to a bowl and add the sliced chicken, fish sauce, and sugar, stirring to mix well. Squeeze the water out of the banana flower and lay the flower on the banana leaf pieces, then the basil leaves and the chicken on top. Fold the leaves to form a package and seal with cocktail sticks. (If you use foil, wrap to create a package.) Steam for 20 minutes and serve. Garnish with sliced chile and coconut milk.

Hot
Serves 4 as part of a Thai meal
Preparation and cooking time: 40 minutes

Family restaurants serving local food are open all day throughout Thailand.

steamed fish with vegetables and spicy sauce

pla nung jeew

Isan-style steamed fish has a clean, fresh taste, popular in the cooler weather when the temperature drops to 50°F (10°C), which is very cold by local standards. Use sole or any other firm, white fish suitable for steaming.

Steamed Vegetable and Fish
  Dipping Sauce (see pages
  138–139)
1 lb 9 oz (700 g) white fish
  filets (or 1 whole fish, cleaned
  and scaled)
3½ oz (100 g) Chinese cabbage,
  including leaves for steaming
  the fish
1 lemongrass stalk, finely sliced
Handful of Thai sweet basil
⅔ cup (80 g) green beans, sliced
  into 2.5-cm (1-in) pieces
3 carrots, peeled and chopped
  into 1-in (2.5-cm) slices
¼ cup (50 g) broccoli
½ cup (50 g) baby corn
2 zucchini, sliced into
  matchsticks
Lettuce leaves and cucumber
  slices, to serve

Make the sauce and set aside to cool.

Rinse the fish and pat dry. Arrange some of the Chinese cabbage leaves on a plate, place the lemongrass and sweet basil on to the cabbage, and lay the fish on top. (If you are using one whole fish, stuff the lemongrass and sweet basil into the cavity.)

Bring water to a boil in the bottom half of a steamer, place the plate in it, cover, and steam for 15–18 minutes. After 10 minutes, add the vegetables to be cooked, or steam them separately if it is more convenient. Both the fish and the vegetables must be piping hot when you serve them with the spicy sauce. Add lettuce leaves and cucumber slices to serve.

Hot
Serves 4 as part of a Thai meal
Preparation and cooking time: 1 hour

crying tiger
suer roong hai

This is a very special dish from Isan. Legend has it that it owes its name to a time when the many tigers that roamed the thick forests there would come to the villages in search of food, especially cattle. The first tiger would take the best part of the meat, then the second tiger would discover this and cry loudly because it had missed out. Some people also say that the grilling meat makes a noise like a crying tiger—whichever version you favor, the dish is irresistible.

MARINADE
2 teaspoons soy sauce
1 teaspoon oyster sauce
1 teaspoon chili powder
1 teaspoon ground white
  pepper
1 teaspoon superfine sugar
1 teaspoon finely chopped garlic

10 oz (300 g) beef, such as
  sirloin
Lettuce leaves, cucumber slices,
  slices of chile, cherry tomatoes,
  cilantro, and mint leaves,
  to serve
½ cup (100 ml) Isan Chili
  Sauce (see page 139)

Mix all the marinade ingredients together. Marinate for at least 2 hours in the refrigerator.

Broil or grill the beef until medium-rare, or to your taste, then slice into strips and serve with lettuce, cucumber, slices of chile, cherry tomatoes, cilantro, mint leaves, and the chili sauce on the side.

Hot
Serves 4 as part of a Thai meal
Marinating: 2 hours Preparation and cooking time: 25 minutes

Offering alms to the monks is an integral part of the Thai people's daily life.

shrimp with chiles, lime, and bitter melon

goong chea num pla

The chilled shrimp and bitter melon complement the fiery hot sauce in this Thai favorite. Other varieties of melon won't work in this recipe because they are too sweet, so substitute cucumber slices if bitter melon is not available.

7 oz (200 g) small to
  medium–size fresh raw shrimp,
  in the shell
1 bitter melon, sliced

SAUCE
Juice of 4 limes
3½ tablespoons fish sauce
1 teaspoon superfine sugar
5 chiles, finely chopped
6 garlic cloves, finely chopped,
  plus 1, sliced, to garnish
2 tablespoons finely chopped
  cilantro
Whole cilantro leaves, to
  garnish

Shell the shrimp, vein, and remove the heads, but leave the tails on. Rinse the shrimp in cold water, put on a plate, cover with plastic wrap, and place in the refrigerator to chill.

To make the sauce, mix the lime juice, fish sauce, and sugar in a bowl, then add the chopped chiles, garlic, and cilantro. Arrange the melon slices on a plate, add the chilled shrimp, and spoon the sauce over them. Garnish with cilantro leaves.

Very hot
Serves 4 as part of a Thai meal
Preparation and cooking time: 30 minutes

Glimpse of a Buddha through the lotus flowers at a shrine.

Northern Thailand

Creamy noodles & green chili dipping sauces

The north of Thailand is mountainous and very fertile, a beautiful area of teak-forested mountainsides, misty valleys, pagodalike temples, and, of course, Thai elephants. This is a meeting place of many cultures, the site of the first kingdoms of Siam. Influences from Myanmar are strong, and nomadic hill tribes, identifiable by their decorative and individual style of dress, inhabit the high mountain areas.

Chiang Mai is the busy cultural and culinary center where visitors base themselves for mountain treks or adventurous car tours. Driving to Chiang Rai near the Laos border, we passed countless little farms growing fruit and vegetables, with ducks, chickens, and pigs scratching around in the yards. Stalls along the way sell coconut-based sweet cakes and, one of my childhood favorites, freshly roasted coconuts—whole coconuts roasted over a fire and cracked open to reveal flesh with a nutty, smoky flavor.

Two of the most famous local dishes are *Gaeng Hanglay* (see pages 92–93), a Burmese curry, and *Khao Soi* noodles (see pages 94–95), a delicious, multicultural hybrid. Like regional dishes anywhere in the world, there is a basic style for these recipes, but individual cooks take pride in their own variations. *Gaeng Hanglay* is a favorite centerpiece for celebrations and important occasions and, rather like a roast chicken or turkey with all the trimmings in the West, there are countless

Early morning in the mountains between Mae Hong Song and Chiang Rai, Northern Thailand.

permutations—everyone has his or her own way of preparing it, adding ingredients according to taste.

Ginger, turmeric, and galangal are the basic flavorings in *Gaeng Hanglay*, which is traditionally made with pork or chicken, although I have made it with beef for this book. For *Khao Soi*, fresh egg noodles are mixed with a creamy sauce and ground pork or the area's flavorsome chicken. I am a huge fan of Chiang Mai Chicken Salad (see pages 86–87), a shredded chicken salad with a spicy sauce, which is all the more delicious because the local chicken tastes just how I think chicken should.

Chiang Mai is also famous for its pork and for sausage-making. For me, the smell of grilling freshly made *Sai Ouar* sausages (see pages 100–101), seasoned with turmeric, lemongrass, chiles, and black pepper, is totally irresistible. *Nem Sor* (see pages 98–99) is another favorite, a great snack of rice balls flavored with pork, chiles, mint, and lime.

The relatively cool climate and rainfall create good growing conditions for almost anything, from tropical fruits and vegetables to cooler-climate varieties. The region's plentiful vegetables are eaten raw or blanched and served with a series of dipping sauces such as *Nam Prik Noom* (see pages 90–91), a thick, pounded chili dip made with green chiles and eaten with vegetables and sticky rice. *Nam Prik Ong* (see pages 88–89) is a thick, spicy dipping sauce made with pork and eaten with fresh vegetables and sticky rice.

As a visitor to the region, you will almost certainly enjoy a *khan tok* meal, sitting on the floor around a low table eating a range of Northern dishes served in small bowls. Northern dishes are generally less fiery than those of Isan, except for potent dipping sauces such as *Nam Prik Noom*, which you will need to tailor carefully to your taste when making it at home.

Evening prayers at Wat Phra That Doi Suthep, Chiang Mai.

chiang mai chicken salad
yum jin gai

Yum Jin Gai in the Northern country dialect means shredded chicken salad with hot and spicy sauce, and the best are made with tasty, free-range chicken.

10 oz (300 g) skinless, boneless
  chicken breasts
2¼ cups (500 ml) Coconut Milk
  (see page 16)
1 teaspoon ground turmeric
½ teaspoon salt

SAUCE
3 tablespoons fish sauce
1 tablespoon fresh lime juice
1½ teaspoons palm sugar
1½ teaspoons chili powder, or
  to taste
1 lemongrass stalk, finely sliced
4 shallots, thinly sliced
2 scallions, finely chopped
15 mint leaves
1 tablespoon cilantro leaves
Cucumber slices peeled
  lengthwise and whole, dried
  chiles, to serve

Place the chicken breasts in a saucepan, cover with coconut milk, and add the turmeric. Bring to a boil, reduce the heat, and simmer until the chicken is done, about 15 minutes. Remove and set aside to drain and cool, then tear the chicken into small pieces, add salt, mix well, and set the chicken aside while you prepare the sauce.

In a bowl, mix the fish sauce, lime juice, and palm sugar, then add the chicken, chili powder, lemongrass, sliced shallots, scallions, mint leaves, and cilantro. Mix well until the chicken is coated with the sauce and serve with cucumber and dried chiles.

Medium-hot
Serves 4 as part of a Thai meal
Preparation and cooking time: 30 minutes

Dating from 1476, Wat Phra That Lampang Luang is one of Northern Thailand's earliest and most impressive temples.

pork and herb dipping sauce
nam prik ong

This classic, spicy dipping sauce recipe is from the Chiang Mai region. It is always included in celebrations and festivals, when people traditionally sit on the floor and enjoy a range of dishes eaten with sticky rice.

4 slices galangal, finely chopped

8 dried chiles, seeded and soaked in warm water

5 garlic cloves, peeled and chopped

1½ shallots, finely chopped

½ teaspoon salt

1 teaspoon shrimp paste

15 cherry tomatoes, halved

2 tablespoons vegetable oil

10½ oz (300 g) ground pork or chicken

2 tablespoons water

½ tablespoon Tamarind Juice (see pages 16–17)

½ tablespoon fish sauce

3 teaspoons superfine sugar

Fresh vegetables, such as lettuce, cucumber, Thai eggplants, Chinese cabbage leaves, steamed green beans, to serve

2 cilantro leaves, to garnish

Using a mortar and pestle, pound the galangal, chiles, garlic, shallots, salt, and shrimp paste, then transfer to a mixing bowl. Add the cherry tomatoes and mix together well.

Heat the oil in a wok, add the pounded paste, and cook until golden brown. Add the pork and cook for a further 10 minutes. Reduce the heat, add the water, tamarind juice, fish sauce, and sugar, and simmer for 5 minutes, stirring often, until the dip thickens.

Serve in a bowl with the fresh vegetables arranged on a plate beside it, ready for dipping, and garnish with cilantro.

Medium-hot
Serves 4 as part of a Thai meal
Preparation and cooking time: 30 minutes

Colorful temple offerings at a festival in Chiang Mai.

pounded green chili dip
nam prik noom

Translated literally, this means "young, unripe chiles made for dipping." Only use green chiles for this—you'll need some small and some large to balance the spicy taste. If you want this very hot, use only small chiles; for a milder taste, use only large green chiles.

3½ oz (100 g) small green,
  unripe chiles
5 large green chiles
5 shallots, unpeeled
12 garlic cloves, unpeeled
3 medium tomatoes
4 Thai eggplants
2 tablespoons fish sauce
2 tablespoons fresh lime juice
1 teaspoon palm sugar
1 tablespoon finely chopped
  shallot
Slices of chile

Broil the chiles, whole shallots, garlic, tomatoes, and eggplants under medium heat until the skins brown, about 7 minutes. Leave to cool. When cool enough to handle, peel off the skins.

Halve the tomatoes and eggplants, then, using a mortar and pestle, pound the tomatoes, eggplants, chiles, shallots, and garlic to a fine paste. Transfer the paste to a bowl and add the fish sauce, lime juice, and palm sugar, mixing well until the sugar dissolves.

Sprinkle the dip with chopped shallot and slices of chile and serve with grilled meat, Chiang Mai Northern Sausage (see pages 100–101), sticky rice, fresh or steamed vegetables, or pork crackers (see page 16). This dip can be kept in an airtight, sterilized jar in the refrigerator for two or three weeks (see page 14).

Medium-hot
Serves 4 as part of a Thai meal
Preparation and cooking time: 1 hour

Main Buddha at Wat Mahathat, Sukhothai.

northern-style beef curry
gaeng hanglay

Traders and teak loggers from Myanmar introduced this rich and fragrant curry to Chiang Mai, originally using fatty pork without coconut milk to make the dish and eating it with plenty of rice to give them energy. Today, *Gaeng Hanglay* is made in many different ways and is a delicacy often served in large quantities for special occasions. Beef simmered in coconut milk gives the curry a rich flavor.

2½ cups (600 ml) Coconut Milk
   (see page 16)
Gaeng Hanglay Paste (see
   page 14)
1 lb 10 oz (800 g) beef, such as
   flank or skirt, cut into chunks
1¼ cups (300 ml) water
1 tablespoon soy sauce
2 tablespoons fish sauce
2 tablespoons Tamarind Juice
   (see pages 16–17)
2 tablespoons roasted, unsalted
   peanuts
2 tablespoons finely sliced
   gingerroot
½ tablespoon palm sugar
Whole, fresh chiles to garnish

Place 1¼ cups (300 ml) of the coconut milk in a flameproof casserole dish and heat over medium heat until it boils, then add the *Gaeng Hanglay* paste and simmer until the oil separates and rises to the surface, about 8 to 10 minutes. Add the beef, stirring to mix well. Simmer, uncovered, for about 20 minutes, then add the remaining coconut milk and the water. Bring back to a boil and simmer until the beef is tender, about 2 hours.

Add the other ingredients, stir well to mix, garnish, and serve with rice.

Spicy
Serves 4 as part of a Thai meal
Preparation and cooking time: 3 hours

The Karen (Kariang) hill-tribe people, originally from Myanmar.

chiang mai noodles
khao soi

One of the most popular noodle dishes from the Northern region, originally introduced by the Chinese Haw people, Chiang Mai Noodles combine a rich, creamy sauce with the softness of boiled noodles and the contrasting crunchiness of the crispy-fried ones that are used as a garnish. Use fresh egg noodles for the best results.

Scant 1 cup (200 ml) vegetable
  oil, for deep-frying
10 oz (300 g) fresh thin egg
  noodles
1¾ cups (400 ml) Coconut Milk
  (see page 16)
1 tablespoon Chiang Mai
  Noodle Paste (see page 15)
4 oz (120 g) skinless, boneless
  chicken breast, sliced
1 tablespoon medium curry
  powder
1¾ cups (400 ml) Chicken Stock
  (see page 138)
2 tablespoons fish sauce
1 tablespoon soy sauce
6¼ cups (1½ L) water
1 teaspoon chili powder
2 scallions, finely sliced
8 cilantro leaves
Crispy-fried chiles
1 lime, quartered

Heat the oil in a deep, heavy-bottomed saucepan and deep-fry 2 oz (50 g) of the noodles until crispy. Remove, drain, and set aside to use as garnish.

Heat scant 1 cup (200 ml) of the coconut milk in a saucepan and add the paste, stirring for a minute or so until the paste oil separates and rises to the surface. Add the chicken and simmer for 5 minutes, then add the curry powder, followed by the remaining coconut milk and the chicken stock. Season with the fish sauce and soy sauce and simmer for a further 10 minutes, or until the chicken is done.

Reduce the heat to very low to keep the chicken warm. Bring the water to a boil in a separate saucepan and cook the remaining fresh egg noodles for about 1 minute, then stir and drain. Transfer the noodles to individual bowls, pour over the chicken and coconut milk sauce, and top with crispy noodles. Sprinkle over a little chili powder, sliced scallions, cilantro leaves, and crispy-fried chiles, and serve each portion with a wedge of lime.

Spicy
Serves 4 as part of a Thai meal
Preparation and cooking time: 1 hour

sukhothai noodles
guay teow sukhothai

Unlike many noodle recipes, which are quick to prepare, this one takes a few hours because the soup is made from scratch. Timing the noodles and the final additions to the soup is important if you want to serve this hot—Thailand is a tropical country where food doesn't need to be hot when served, but elsewhere there will be a need for a warming bowl of delicious noodles on a cold winter's day. Roasted chili powder, chopped peanuts, fried garlic, and an extra spoonful of sugar are favorite Thai additions.

2 lb 4 oz (1 kg) pork leg bone

13 cups (3 L) water

4 garlic cloves, peeled

2 cilantro roots

1 teaspoon salt

2 teaspoons dried shrimp

14 oz (400 g) pork filet

2 teaspoons ground white pepper

3 tablespoons fish sauce

1 tablespoon soy sauce

1 tablespoon superfine sugar

4 tablespoons vegetable oil

1 tablespoon chopped garlic

6¼ cups (1½ L) water, for boiling the noodles

13 oz (375 g) medium rice stick noodles, soaked in warm water for about 15 minutes

¾ cup (100 g) snake beans (or green beans)

1½ cups (150 g) bean sprouts

2 tablespoons finely chopped cilantro

2 tablespoons finely chopped scallion

Wash the pork bone, put it in a large stockpot, and pour over the water. Bring to a boil, then add the whole garlic cloves, cilantro roots, salt, and dried shrimp. Reduce the heat a little and simmer for 3 hours, skimming every so often to remove the scum that rises to the surface.

Add the pork filet to the stockpot and cook until it is done, but not breaking up—this takes about 30 minutes. Remove the meat and set aside to cool, then cut into slices about 1 in (2.5 cm) thick. Add the white pepper, fish sauce, soy sauce, and sugar to the stock and continue to simmer.

Heat the vegetable oil in a skillet and fry the chopped garlic until golden brown, then remove the skillet from the heat immediately to avoid burning the garlic. Set aside the garlic-flavored oil to add to the noodles when you are ready to serve.

Bring the water for cooking the noodles to a boil in a saucepan, add the noodles, and stir to prevent sticking. Cook for about 3 minutes, until just soft (don't overcook them). Remove, drain, and divide the noodles equally among four bowls.

Meanwhile, bring the soup back to a boil, add the snake beans, and cook for 2 minutes, then add the bean sprouts and cook for a further 30 seconds. Lift out the beans and bean sprouts and place on one side of the noodles. Arrange the pork slices on the other side, add ladlefuls of soup and the garlic oil, and stir in the chopped cilantro and scallion. Garnish and serve with Chili Vinegar (see page 141).

Spicy
Serves 4 as part of a Thai meal
Preparation and cooking time: 4 hours

deep-fried rice balls with chiles and lime

nem sor

Some people claim this is a Vietnamese dish, while others insist it is a Northern Thai dish. Either way, it makes a wonderful snack. *Nem* is a local word for preserved pork (pork, pork skin, garlic, chiles, and salt, wrapped in banana leaves to preserve it). Here, ground pork is used, to translate the recipe for home cooking. Don't be put off by the pork skin— it gives a more authentic flavor.

2½ cups (200 g) cooked rice

2 kaffir lime leaves, finely sliced

1 tablespoon Red Curry Paste
  (see page 15)

½ cup (50 g) shredded coconut

1 teaspoon salt

3 tablespoons all-purpose flour

7 tablespoons water

2¼ cups (500 ml) vegetable oil,
  for deep-frying, plus
  2 tablespoons for cooking the
  ground pork

7 oz (200 g) ground pork

2½ tablespoons fresh lime juice

2 tablespoons fish sauce

1 teaspoon sugar

2 oz (50 g) cooked, Shredded
  Pork Skin (see page 16)

2 tablespoons finely chopped
  scallions

3 shallots, finely sliced

Handful of mint leaves

16 crispy-fried chiles, lettuce,
  and cilantro leaves, to garnish

Mix the rice with the lime leaves, red curry paste, shredded coconut, and ½ teaspoon of the salt in a bowl and, using your hands, form the mixture into 6 golfball-size balls. In another bowl, mix the flour and water together to make a batter, then roll the balls in it to coat them. Heat the oil for deep-frying in a deep, heavy-bottomed skillet and deep-fry the rice balls for 3–4 minutes, until golden brown. Remove, drain, and set aside to cool.

Heat 2 tablespoons oil in a wok and cook the ground pork until it is done, about 5 minutes. In a separate bowl, combine the lime juice, fish sauce, and sugar and mix until the sugar dissolves. Add the cooked ground pork, shredded pork skin, scallions, shallots, and the rice balls, roughly broken up into pieces. Add the mint leaves and mix together, then serve garnished with crispy-fried chiles, lettuce leaves, and cilantro. Make extra rice balls to serve whole, if you wish.

Medium-hot
Makes 6
Preparation and cooking time: 1 hour 30 minutes

Painting on the wall of the Wat Phra That Lampang Luang.

chiang mai northern sausage
sai ouar

This is the traditional lean and tasty pork sausage of Northern Thailand spiced with black pepper, chili, and turmeric. In Chiang Mai, you find them being freshly broiled—the smell is irresistible, and Thais buy them to eat with the equally irresistible steamed sticky rice.

4 lemongrass stalks, finely
  chopped

1 tablespoon chili powder

8 garlic cloves, peeled and finely
  chopped

4 shallots, peeled and finely
  chopped

4 cilantro roots

1 lb 2 oz (500 g) ground pork
  with some fat

4 teaspoons sea salt

4 teaspoons superfine sugar

8 tablespoons chopped
  cilantro

1 teaspoon freshly ground black
  pepper

4 teaspoons chopped galangal

1 teaspoon ground turmeric

4 kaffir lime leaves, finely sliced

12 sausage casings (bought from
  the butcher)

Using a mortar and pestle, pound the lemongrass, chili powder, garlic, shallots, and cilantro roots to a fine paste.

In a bowl, combine the ground pork with all the remaining ingredients (except the sausage casings) and mix well. Stuff the sausage casings evenly with the mixture to make about 12 sausages.

Prick the sausages with a fork and grill, broil, or fry. This is delicious served with sticky rice, lettuce, chiles, cashew nuts, and scallions.

Spicy
Serves 4 as part of a Thai meal
Preparation and cooking time: 1 hour

Grilled sausages sizzling in the Chiang Mai markets.

The South
Seafood & spice

My memories of visits to the exotic south of Thailand are of smiling faces, the relaxed atmosphere, the beautiful turquoise color of the sea, and, not surprisingly for an area with two such lengthy coastlines, the sensational fresh seafood.

Platters of shellfish, such as huge, juicy shrimp, crabs, and lobster; large bowls of yellow fish curry made with pungent spices and coconut; and bright fruits and vegetables, all served against the backdrop of the sea, are signature images of Southern Thailand. Apart from the visual impact, the tastes are particular to the South—salty from the shrimp paste and fish sauce used in happy abundance, hot with chiles, and pungent with spices that were originally introduced by coastal traders.

Less sweet than the dishes of Central Thailand, curries here are invariably yellow through the addition of turmeric or saffron and some are spiced with cinnamon, cardamom, or cloves. All of these signify a Southern dish. *Gaeng Mussaman* (see pages 114–115) is a famous example, a particularly spicy, rich curry that we make with potatoes and beef shank at the Arun Thai to withstand the long cooking time. This dish may take some practice to balance all of the tastes to your liking. *Gaeng Leung Pla* (see pages 112–113) is the local spicy yellow fish curry made with a range of vegetables, and *Khao Mok Gai* (see pages 120–121) is a chicken curry made with cinnamon, cloves, and turmeric, and served with saffron rice.

The recipes I have included here for dishes such as Steamed Mussels with Lemongrass and Sweet Basil (see

Sunset over the Ko Hai rock islands in the Andaman Sea near Trang.

pages 118–119), Chicken Soup with Lime and Turmeric (see pages 106–107), and Hot and Sour Yellow Fish Curry (see pages 112–113) will give you an immediate insight into the Southern style.

Visiting Southern Thailand, you might find some of the favorite tastes surprising, such as the prized durian, a fruit that smells terrible but tastes delicious. Signs on hotel doors will warn you that this fruit is not to be brought inside. The large, bitter twisted or stink (*sator*) beans are another Southern favorite, and I have included the recipe for *Goong Pad Sator* (see pages 116–117), where they are paired with stir-fried shrimp, because it is an important part of Southern cuisine. For me, memories of the South also include mackerel steamed in a basket and sold cooked in every market. Once plentiful, this is now more of a specialty dish. The same goes for bird's nests, generally believed in Asia to have health-giving and aphrodisiac properties. They are traditionally collected by gypsies living in thatched huts near the water, who collect the empty nests by using ladders to scale the cliffs.

During our visits for research and photography for this book, photographer Ken Martin and I flew from Bangkok to Trang to begin our first journey around the South. We drove through the rubber plantations to Pak Meng on the west coast and pulled up under the casuarina trees at a restaurant beside the beach. The owner brought snacks and beers, and, of course, we talked about local food, what was available, and, specifically, what we would like to eat that evening. Watching people wade out to net the shellfish fresh for dinner was, for me, the very essence of the Thai experience—Thai people welcome you to their homes, and their restaurants will always serve you the very best of what they have available.

Fishing villages like this one at Pak Meng supply the daily seafood markets.

chicken soup with lime and turmeric

gai tom kha min

This soup isn't so much spicy as rich from the stock and earthy from the turmeric. Balanced with lime and fish sauce, this classic dish from Southern Thailand is especially good made with corn-fed or free-range chicken.

2 garlic cloves, peeled

2 shallots, peeled and finely sliced

1-in (2.5-cm) piece fresh turmeric root or 1 teaspoon ground turmeric

3 cups (750 ml) Chicken Stock (see page 138)

1 cup (250 ml) Coconut Milk (see page 16)

4 kaffir lime leaves, torn

7 oz (200 g) skinless, boneless chicken breasts, cut into fine strips

4 tablespoons fish sauce

2½ tablespoons fresh lime juice

1 teaspoon superfine sugar

8 baby corn cobs

4 field mushrooms, quartered

8 crispy-fried chiles and cilantro leaves, to garnish

Using a mortar and pestle, pound the garlic, sliced shallots, and turmeric to a fine paste.

Heat the chicken stock and coconut milk in a medium saucepan, then add the paste, kaffir lime leaves, and chicken strips and boil together for 8–10 minutes.

Add the fish sauce, lime juice, and sugar to the soup, then add the baby corn and mushrooms. Simmer for about 2 minutes, then serve immediately. Garnish with crispy-fried chiles and cilantro leaves.

Spicy
Serves 4 as part of a Thai meal
Preparation and cooking time: 30 minutes

Growers bring their fresh herbs and vegetables to the morning markets every day at Surat Thani on the Gulf of Thailand.

crispy fish with tai pla sauce

gaeng Tai pla

Tai Pla is an infamously pungent, salty sauce made from fish innards fermented in barrels with salt for over a year. You don't have to make the sauce—just look for a bottle at your local Asian grocery store.

1 teaspoon shrimp paste

6 garlic cloves, peeled

1 lemongrass stalk, finely chopped

4 small red chiles, chopped

1 teaspoon grated lime rind

1 teaspoon ground turmeric

3¾ cups (800 ml) Fish Stock (see page 138)

3 tablespoons *tai pla* sauce

1 cup (100 g) bamboo shoots

¾ cup (100 g) green beans

½ cup (50 g) Thai eggplants or twisted beans (*sator*)

3 teaspoons superfine sugar

6 kaffir lime leaves, torn

13½ oz (400 g) fish, such as sole or flounder, deep-fried

Put the shrimp paste in a foil package and roast for 8 minutes at 325°F (160°C). Using a mortar and pestle, pound the garlic, lemongrass, chopped chiles, grated lime rind, and turmeric until fine, then mix in the roasted shrimp paste.

Put the fish stock in a medium saucepan and bring to a boil, then add the *tai pla* sauce and the pounded paste. Cook for about 4 minutes, then add the bamboo shoots, green beans, and Thai eggplants. Add the sugar and torn kaffir lime leaves. Cook until the vegetables are tender but still crisp to the bite, then add the deep-fried fish, stir well, and cook briefly, until the fish is heated through.

Very hot
Serves 4 as part of a Thai meal
Preparation and cooking time: 1 hour

Fish drying on nets in the sun at a fishing village in Phuket.

lamb in yellow curry

gaeng khari gae

This is our special recipe, cooked for 17 years in our two restaurants. It was created by Ell, one of our respected curry chefs who lived in Southern Thailand for a long time, and who brings the best traditions of old Southern cuisine to our kitchens. This recipe also works well with meats such as venison or wild boar.

Scant 1 cup (200 ml) coconut cream

2 tablespoons Red Curry Paste (see page 15)

1 lb 12 oz (800 g) lean leg of lamb, boned and cut into chunks

3¾ cups (800 ml) Coconut Milk (see page 16)

2 onions, roughly chopped

1 teaspoon ground turmeric

1 tablespoon medium or hot yellow curry powder with a high turmeric content

6 tablespoons fish sauce

3 tablespoons palm sugar

12 small potatoes

4 small onions

Cilantro leaves, sliced, fresh chiles, and fried shallots to garnish

Cucumber Relish (see page 141)

Heat the coconut cream in a large saucepan over low heat, add the red curry paste, and cook, stirring until the curry paste oil separates and rises to the surface.

Add the chunks of lamb and mix together well, add the coconut milk and bring to a boil, then add the chopped onion and simmer (uncovered) for 3 hours, until the meat is tender.

Add the turmeric, curry powder, fish sauce, palm sugar, potatoes, and small onions and cook until the potatoes are tender. Garnish and serve with the cucumber relish.

Medium-hot
Serves 4 as part of a Thai meal
Preparation and cooking time: About 4 hours

Bargaining for the best price for the day's supplies.

hot and sour yellow fish curry

gaeng leung pla

One of the most popular Southern yellow curries, this dish is extremely hot, spicy, and sour. The locals use this method to prepare a wide range of seafood, including the impressively large jumbo shrimp that are found in the area, and all sorts of vegetables. This is a liquid-style curry to be eaten with plain rice.

1 teaspoon shrimp paste

10 red chiles or to taste, chopped

1-in (2.5-cm) piece fresh turmeric root, peeled and finely chopped (or 1 teaspoon ground turmeric)

5 garlic cloves, peeled and chopped

4 shallots, peeled and chopped

4½ cups (1 L) Fish Stock (see page 138)

1 lb 5 oz (600 g) white fish filets, cut into chunks

7 oz (200 g) Chinese cabbage leaves

1½ cups (150 g) sliced bamboo shoots

1½ cups (150 g) broccoli or cauliflower florets

7 tablespoons fish sauce

4 tablespoons fresh lime juice

4 tablespoons Tamarind Juice (see pages 16–17)

Wrap the shrimp paste in a foil package and roast at 325°F (160°C) for about 5–7 minutes, until it is dry. Take care not to burn it.

Using a mortar and pestle, pound the chiles, turmeric, garlic, and shallots until fine. Add the roasted shrimp paste and mix together.

Heat the fish stock in a large saucepan, add the pounded ingredients, and boil for 5 minutes, then add the fish and cook for about 7 minutes, until the fish is done. Add the cabbage, bamboo shoots, and broccoli or cauliflower florets and cook until they are tender, about 7 minutes, then season with fish sauce, lime juice, and tamarind juice. Serve hot.

Very hot
Serves 4 as part of a Thai meal
Preparation and cooking time: 40 minutes

Longtail speedboats waiting to take tourists to the rock islands at Phi Phi.

mussaman beef curry

gaeng mussaman

This is a spicy Southern Thai curry with Islamic origins. Portuguese traders brought turmeric, cinnamon, cumin, cloves, and nutmeg from the Middle East and India to the south coast of Thailand and the Gulf of Siam at roughly the same time as they brought chili. This recipe combines these dry spices with Thai sweet, sour, and salty tastes. I use a stewing cut of beef, because the curry needs to be boiled for up to four hours.

6¼ cups (1½ L) Coconut Milk
(see page 16)
3½ oz (100 g) Mussaman Curry
Paste (see page 16)
2 lb 4 oz (1 kg) beef, flank or
skirt, cut into 1-in (2.5-cm)
pieces
Handful of dried bay leaves (or
6–7 fresh bay leaves)
12 small potatoes suitable for
stewing, peeled (or larger
potatoes, peeled and
quartered)
8 baby onions, peeled
5½ tablespoons fish sauce
3 tablespoons palm sugar
7 tablespoons Tamarind Juice
(see pages 16–17)
Fried onions, cilantro leaves,
and slices of chile, to garnish

Heat scant 1 cup (200 ml) of the coconut milk in a large saucepan and add the mussaman paste, stirring together until the oil from the paste separates and rises to the surface.

Add the beef, stirring well to combine with the coconut milk mixture, then add the bay leaves and the remaining coconut milk and simmer for 3 hours, until the beef is tender.

Add the potatoes and onions and simmer for a further hour, until the potatoes are cooked. Season the curry with fish sauce, palm sugar, and tamarind juice. Garnish with some fried onions, cilantro leaves, and slices of chile.

Spicy
Serves 4 as part of a Thai meal
Preparation and cooking time: 4 hours

Exotic, tropical fruits like mangosteen, green mango, and rambutan are delicious served after a spicy Thai curry.

stir-fried shrimp with sator beans

goong pad sator

Thai people in the Southern region love the taste of their pungent *sator*—large, flat beans with a strong smell and a bitter taste. Frozen *sator* beans are exported around the world to keep homesick Thais, who find the flavor delicious, happy. These beans are something of an acquired taste, like strong blue cheese— you either love them, smell included, or loathe them.

3 cloves garlic, peeled

3 small red chiles

1 teaspoon shrimp paste

1 tablespoon vegetable oil

8 raw jumbo shrimp, shelled
  and veined

¾ cup (100 g) twisted or
  stink beans (*sator*)

1 tablespoon Chicken Stock (see
  page 138)

2 long red chiles, sliced

1½ tablespoons fish sauce

1 tablespoon oyster sauce

1 teaspoon superfine sugar

3 kaffir lime leaves

Using a mortar and pestle, pound the garlic, chiles, and shrimp paste together to form a fine paste.

Heat the oil in a wok, add the paste, and cook briefly until it releases its aroma. Add the shrimp and cook for 3 minutes. Add the beans, stock, and sliced chiles and mix well. Cook for a further 2–3 minutes.

Season with fish sauce, oyster sauce, and sugar and cook for a further 2 minutes. Add the kaffir lime leaves and serve with plain rice.

Hot
Serves 4 as part of a Thai meal
Preparation and cooking time: 20 minutes

Twisted (sator) beans are shelled and added to stir-fries and curries, and can also be eaten raw with dipping sauce.

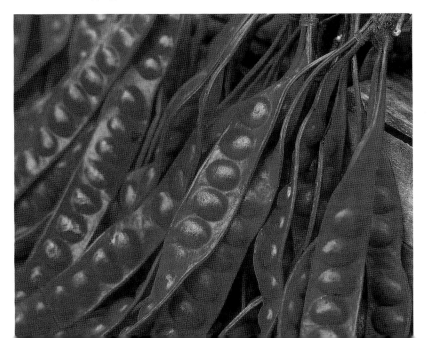

steamed mussels with lemongrass and sweet basil

hoi maleang phu neung ta-khrai

Mussels in Thailand are small and tasty. The little ones are best for this recipe, where they are steamed and served with a pungent seafood sauce.

1 lb 12 oz (800 g) fresh mussels, in the shell
3 garlic cloves, peeled
3 small red chiles
1 lemongrass stalk, sliced
1 kaffir lime leaf, torn
⅔ cup (150 ml) Fish Stock (see page 138)
½ teaspoon salt
Handful of Thai sweet basil leaves
Seafood Sauce (see page 140)

Put the mussels in a large pot of cold water and use a brush to scrub and beard them, removing the hairy growth from the shell. Drain and rinse the mussels in clean water. Discard any that fail to close when tapped sharply.

Using a mortar and pestle, pound the garlic and chiles together to form a fine paste. Transfer the paste to a large saucepan and add the mussels, lemongrass, kaffir lime leaf, fish stock, and salt. Steam for about 6 minutes, until the mussels open (discard any that fail to open), transfer to a bowl, garnish with basil leaves, and serve with the seafood sauce.

Medium-hot
Serves 4 as part of a Thai meal
Preparation and cooking time: 25 minutes

Buddhas covered in gleaming gold-leaf.

saffron rice with chicken
khao mok gai

Dishes featuring saffron rice originate from Southern Thailand. *Khao Mok Gai* is often cooked in a big pot and served at special family occasions such as weddings and other religious ceremonies. Guests traditionally sit on the floor and eat this dish as part of a feast that usually includes a fish or meat curry. If you prefer, substitute ground turmeric for the saffron.

2¼ cups (500 ml) vegetable oil, for deep-frying, plus extra for stir-frying

2¼ cups (500 g) jasmine rice

½ teaspoon saffron strands (or 1 teaspoon ground turmeric)

3 cups (750 ml) Chicken Stock (see page 138) or water

2 teaspoons salt

½ teaspoon ground white pepper

8 chicken drumsticks

4 cardamom pods

4 fresh bay leaves, torn

2 shallots, peeled, finely sliced, and fried

Slices of chile and cilantro leaves, to garnish

Cucumber Relish (see page 141)

Heat a little oil in a wok and stir-fry the rice with the saffron to mix together, then add the stock. Season with the salt and pepper, cover, and cook for 10 minutes.

Heat the oil and deep-fry the chicken drumsticks until the skin is golden brown, about 5 minutes. Remove the drumsticks, draining carefully, and add to the cooking rice together with the cardamom pods and the torn bay leaves. Boil to reduce the stock, then reduce the heat and simmer for about 20 minutes until the rice is cooked and all the liquid has been absorbed.

Sprinkle the fried shallots, sliced chile, and cilantro leaves over the chicken and rice and serve with cucumber relish.

Mild
Serves 4 as part of a Thai meal
Preparation and cooking time: 35 minutes

Tasty native chickens grilling Thai-style over charcoal.

Thai "Tapas"
Khap klaem

Snacks and appetizers to go with drinks are called *khap klaem*, literally "drinking food," like Spanish tapas. It is a surprising custom in a largely Buddhist country, but very much a part of Thai life, like going to a bar after work in any city.

From the age of five, I lived with my grandfather, grandmother, and two aunties in a two-story house in Isan in Northeastern Thailand. They owned a general store selling everything from clothes to fishing tackle. We had a refrigerator in one corner, the only one in the area, so we had precious ice for cold drinks and sold beer and whisky. There were a few tables outside, and customers would sit and drink while we prepared snacks.

We served betel leaf (*meang khum*), spicy nuts with cilantro and chili, deep-fried snacks (*yum*), Thai salads, and broiled or grilled meat or fish, including satays and Isan sausages. This tradition continues today, and both working men and women stay in town after work to have a drink at bars or corner stores and to eat snacks, before moving on to a restaurant to catch up with friends and family for dinner.

Now we have created our own Thai "tapas" bar here at the Arun Thai restaurant, with a menu of dishes that changes weekly. Recipes for some of the dishes follow in this chapter, and others are scattered throughout the book, such as Crying Tiger beef (see pages 78–79), Stir-Fried Clams with Chile and Basil (see pages 46–47), Isan Duck Salad (see pages 64–65), Shrimp with Chiles, Lime, and Bitter Melon (see pages 80–81), and Chiang Mai Northern Sausage (see pages 100–101).

Thai "tapas" (khap klaem) *are served at the author's Crying Tiger Bar at the Arun Thai restaurant, Sydney.*

shrimp in pastry
goong hom sabai

The name literally means "shrimp with a sash," representing the sash traditionally worn by Thai women on formal occasions. The pastry wrapping takes a bit of practice; don't forget to leave the shrimp tail outside the pastry when you begin to roll it up.

8 uncooked jumbo shrimp,
  shelled
1 tablespoon soy sauce
1 teaspoon superfine sugar
¼ teaspoon ground white
  pepper
6 spring roll sheets
  (10 x 10 in/25 x 25cm)
1 egg yolk, beaten
2¼ cups (500 ml) vegetable oil

PASTE
6 uncooked shrimp
¼ teaspoon ground white
  pepper
½ teaspoon superfine sugar
½ tablespoon soy sauce

Using a sharp knife, score the jumbo shrimp diagonally toward the tail on both sides and horizontally underneath. This will prevent them from curling up as they cook. Mix the soy sauce, sugar, and white pepper in a bowl and add the shrimp to marinate.

Using a blender, mix the paste ingredients together until very fine and set aside.

Cut the spring roll sheets in half diagonally, cutting a slice off one corner and placing that at the center of the sheet. Spread one teaspoon of paste over the pastry piece in the center (this forms an extra layer to prevent moisture seeping through the pastry), then lay a jumbo shrimp on the sheet with the tail outside and roll up tightly, enfolding the shrimp. Seal the edges with beaten egg yolk. Repeat with all the shrimp. Heat the vegetable oil and deep-fry the rolls for 10 minutes. Drain on paper towels. Serve plain or on a bed of crispy-fried noodles and chopped chiles, as shown.

Mild
Makes 8
Preparation and cooking time: 35 minutes

Buddha at Wat Phra That Doi Suthep,
Chiang Mai.

fresh oysters with spicy thai sauce

hoi nang rom sood

Oysters are farmed in the Central and Southern regions of Thailand. The best-known ones, from the Surat Thani area, are large and succulent. Use only the freshest oysters for this recipe.

2 garlic cloves, peeled and very
   finely sliced
1 small red chile, finely sliced
1 shallot, peeled, sliced, and
   crispy-fried
3 tablespoons fresh lime juice
2 tablespoons Chili Sauce (see
   page 139)
24 freshly shucked oysters
Crushed ice
Finely sliced carrot and
   cilantro leaves, to garnish

Place the garlic, chile, shallot, lime juice, and chili sauce into individual little serving dishes.

Arrange the oysters on crushed ice on individual dishes or on a large platter and serve them immediately, because they should be chilled. Garnish with sliced carrot and cilantro leaves. Add a small amount of each ingredient to each oyster in its shell before eating.

Spicy
Serves 4 as part of a Thai meal
Preparation and cooking time: 30 minutes

Wild orchids grow profusely in Northern Thailand.

betel leaves
meang khum

Wrapping these tasty ingredients in crunchy betel nut leaves is a tradition at the Arun Thai—the leaves are seasonal, so customers are always asking when they will be available. In Thailand, Chinese broccoli leaves can also be used, because they share a similar nutty, "grassy" taste that complements the bright flavors of the other ingredients.

SAUCE
1 teaspoon shrimp paste
1 teaspoon vegetable oil
1 teaspoon finely chopped
   galangal (optional)
1 teaspoon finely chopped
   shallot
1 tablespoon finely chopped
   gingerroot
1 teaspoon dried shrimp, finely
   blended
4 tablespoons toasted, shredded
   coconut
5 tablespoons water
3 tablespoons palm sugar
1 tablespoon fish sauce

12 betel nut leaves (or Chinese
   broccoli leaves)
2 tablespoons roasted, unsalted
   peanuts
2 tablespoons dried shrimp
2 tablespoons diced gingerroot
2 tablespoons diced lime (skin on)
2 tablespoons diced shallot
¾ cup (80 g) toasted, shredded
   coconut
2 chiles, sliced into rings

First, make the sauce. Wrap the shrimp paste in foil and broil it for 2–3 minutes, until the paste is dry. Heat the oil in a small saucepan, then add the galangal, shallot, and ginger and stir for 2 minutes to aromatize. Add the dried shrimp, shredded coconut, water, shrimp paste, palm sugar, and fish sauce and stir over low heat until the sauce thickens. The consistency should be quite sticky and the taste both salty and sweet. Remove the sauce from the heat and set aside to cool.

Arrange all the ingredients separately on a serving platter. To serve, spoon on a little of each ingredient on to a betel nut leaf (except the toasted coconut and fresh chile, which are to taste) and top with a teaspoon of the sauce. Wrap the leaf into a bite-size piece and enjoy!

Medium-hot – hot
Serves 4 as part of a Thai meal
Preparation and cooking time: 1 hour

The afternoon markets in Nakhon Pathom sell snacks and selections of ready-cooked food to eat on-the-spot or to take home.

chicken in pandanus leaves
gai hor bai toey

Marinated chicken wrapped in aromatic pandanus leaves makes a wonderful snack or starter. This is the only meat dish made with pandanus leaves in Thailand, because the leaves are usually used for flavoring desserts and sticky rice. They infuse the chicken with their earthy, vanilla aroma and are tied tightly to keep out the oil. The packages must be unwrapped before eating, because pandanus leaves are inedible. Fresh or frozen leaves can be found in specialty Asian food stores.

5 garlic cloves, peeled and finely chopped
4 cilantro roots
1 teaspoon ground white pepper
1 tablespoon superfine sugar
3 tablespoons oyster sauce
2 tablespoons light soy sauce
1 lb 2 oz (500 g) chicken thigh filets, trimmed of fat, each cut into four
12–14 pandanus leaves
2¼ cups (500 ml) vegetable oil for frying
Finely sliced carrot, to garnish

SAUCE
5 tablespoons dark soy sauce
4 tablespoons palm sugar
1 teaspoon white sesame seeds, toasted

Using a mortar and pestle, pound the garlic and cilantro until fine, then transfer to a bowl.

Add the pepper, sugar, oyster sauce, and soy sauce to the bowl. Mix well, making sure the sugar has dissolved, add the chicken, cover, and place in the refrigerator to marinate overnight.

When you are ready to cook, you can wrap the chicken in the pandanus leaves in two ways:

1. Make a triangle with the pandanus leaf, placing the chicken in the center, then wrapping tightly and securing with a cocktail stick.
2. Take a pandanus leaf and twist the left end into the middle of the leaf to create a hollow. Place two of the chicken cubes (1½ x 1½ in/ 4 x 4 cm) in the hollow, then feed the right end through the hole and tighten both ends. Tie tightly so the cooking oil can't seep into the filling, and cut both ends, leaving about 1 in (2.5 cm) at each end.

Make the sauce by simmering the soy sauce and sugar together in a small saucepan, stirring until the palm sugar has dissolved. Transfer to a small bowl for serving, and top with the toasted sesame seeds.

Heat the oil in a heavy-bottomed skillet to 325°F (160°C) and deep-fry the chicken in pandanus leaves for 3–5 minutes. Unwrap the packages and discard the leaves. Check that the chicken is done. Serve the chicken with the sauce. Garnish with sliced carrot.

Mild
Serves 4 as part of a Thai meal
Marinate: Overnight
Preparation and cooking time: 30 minutes

chicken satay
gai satay

Satays are a Malaysian-Indonesian dish from Southern Thailand. Our chicken version is sweet and aromatic from the turmeric and garlic, rather than hot or spicy. This is served with its own satay sauce made with peanuts, coconut milk, and palm sugar. The satays can also be served with Cucumber Relish (see page 141).

1 tablespoon yellow curry
  powder
1 tablespoon chopped garlic
½ teaspoon ground white
  pepper
1 teaspoon ground turmeric
1 teaspoon salt
5 tablespoons superfine sugar
4 tablespoons fish sauce
1 lb 2 oz (500 g) skinless,
  boneless chicken breasts, sliced
  into strips 2½-in (6-cm) long
  and ⅝-in (1½-cm) wide
Coconut Milk (see page 16),
  for brushing
Cucumber strips, sliced raw
  onion, and sliced chile, to
  garnish
Satay Sauce, to serve (see page
  140)

Mix the curry powder, garlic, white pepper, turmeric, salt, sugar, and fish sauce together, add the chicken, cover, and place in the refrigerator to marinate overnight.

Soak wooden skewers in water for 15 minutes to prevent the ends from burning during cooking. Thread the marinated chicken pieces on to the presoaked skewers, brush with coconut milk, and grill or broil for about 3 minutes, until done. Garnish and serve with satay sauce.

Mild
Serves 4 as part of a Thai meal
Marinate: Overnight
Preparation and cooking time: 30 minutes

Street vendors grill their satays on the pavements of Bangkok.

fresh spring rolls

popai sood

Spring rolls are usually served crispy-fried, but these freshly wrapped rolls are an alternative, full of tasty crab, bean sprouts, garlic, cucumber, and tofu. Served with a warm sauce, they make delicious snacks or starters.

OMELET
3 eggs
Pinch of salt
2 teaspoons vegetable oil

SAUCE
1 tablespoon vegetable oil
1 clove garlic, peeled and finely
   chopped
2 teaspoons palm sugar
⅔ cup (150 ml) water
4 tablespoons Tamarind Juice
   (see pages 16–17)
1 long red chile, finely chopped
1 teaspoon salt
2 teaspoons cornstarch dissolved
   in 2 tablespoons water

⅔ cup (150 ml) water
2 garlic cloves, peeled and
   crushed
½ teaspoon salt
3½ oz (100 g) white crabmeat
2 oz (60 g) firm tofu (bean
   curd), cut into 3 x ½-in
   (7½ x 1-cm) pieces
1 cup (60 g) cooked bean sprouts
3 (10 x 10-in/25 x 25-cm) spring
   roll sheets
1 cucumber, cut into 3 x ½-in
   (7½ x 1-cm) strips
Slices of chile and cilantro
   leaves, to garnish

First, make the omelet. Beat the eggs in a bowl and add the salt. Heat the oil in a skillet. Add half the egg mixture and cook until dry on one side, then turn and continue to cook until you have a very thin omelet. Remove from the skillet. Cook the remaining mixture in the same way. When the omelets are cool, slice into thin strips.

Now, make the sauce. Heat the oil in a saucepan, add the garlic, and stir until golden brown. Then, add the sugar, water, tamarind juice, chopped chile, and salt. Stir continuously until the mixture boils. Add the cornstarch and water mixture and mix well, stirring until the sauce thickens. Reduce the heat to keep the sauce just warm while you prepare the spring rolls.

Bring the water to a boil in a saucepan and add the garlic, salt, and crabmeat. Cook for 3 minutes. Remove the crabmeat and set aside to drain, then add the tofu to the liquid and cook for 2 minutes. Remove the tofu and set aside to drain while you cook the bean sprouts in the liquid for 1 minute. Remove and drain.

Remove one spring roll sheet from the bag (they must remain moist), lay it on a flat surface, and spread a third of the omelet slices on top. Add some bean sprouts, tofu, cucumber, and crabmeat and roll up tightly. Cut into four pieces, then repeat with the remaining spring roll sheets. (Reserve a few strips of omelet for garnish.)

Serve immediately, topped with the warm sauce, garnished with slices of chile, cilantro leaves, and thin strips of omelet.

Mild
Serves 4 as part of a Thai meal
Preparation and cooking time: 40 minutes

drunken noodles
pad kee mao

This noodle dish is a favorite in Thai bars and street stalls and is just the thing to enjoy with a drink, or after a drink to sober you up before you go home! Chicken or seafood can be used, but this recipe is made with beef.

10 small red chiles

3 garlic cloves, peeled

4 tablespoons vegetable oil

8 oz (250 g) flat noodles (or thin rice stick noodles)

1 tablespoon dark soy sauce

8 oz (250g) finely sliced beef or ground beef

Handful of holy basil

2 cups (180 g) Chinese broccoli leaves, torn

2 tablespoons sliced onion

2 tablespoons sliced scallion

1 tablespoon light soy sauce

2 tablespoons fish sauce

1 teaspoon superfine sugar

2 tablespoons green peppercorns

Sliced fresh chile, to serve

Pound the chiles and garlic together using a mortar and pestle. Set aside.

Heat 2 tablespoons of the oil in a wok, add the noodles, stir quickly, then add the dark soy sauce and stir well. Remove from the wok and set aside.

Heat the remaining oil in the wok, add the pounded garlic and chili paste, and cook until brown. Then, add the beef and cook, stirring until the beef is done. Now, add the basil leaves, broccoli leaves, onion, scallion, light soy sauce, fish sauce, sugar, and peppercorns. Mix well, then add the noodles, stirring to combine with the sauce, and serve.

Very hot
Serves 4 as part of a Thai meal
Preparation and cooking time: 45 minutes

Clay mortars and wooden pestles are essential Thai utensils.

stocks, sauces, & relishes

Sauces are added to cooked meat and fish, while thicker dipping sauces are actually a dish in their own right made to accompany steamed vegetables, rice, or meat. Thais cook their stocks daily to go with dishes including noodles, stir-fries, meat, vegetables, and seafood, which is another reason why everything tastes so incredibly fresh.

Chicken stock
Makes 4½ cups (1 L)
3 lb (1.5 kg) chicken bones
9 cups (2 L) water
Pinch of salt

Place the bones in the water in a stockpot over high heat and boil for 20 minutes. Skim off the layer of fat that forms, then lower the heat and simmer the stock until the liquid has reduced to almost half. Add the salt, then remove from the heat, and let cool. Strain and discard the bones. This stock will keep in the refrigerator in a sealed container for two weeks.

Fish stock
Makes 4½ cups (1 L)
4½ lb (2 kg) fish heads and bones from fish such as
    snapper, cod, haddock
9 cups (2 L) water
Pinch of salt

Heat a wok, add the fish heads and bones, and fry for 5 minutes, stirring to prevent burning. Then, remove and rinse the bones in boiling water to remove the smell, throwing the water away. In a stockpot, boil the water and add the fish bones. Boil for 5 minutes, then simmer until the stock has reduced by about half. Remove from the heat and cool. Strain and discard the bones. This stock will keep in the refrigerator in a sealed container for two weeks.

Vegetable stock
Makes 4½ cups (1 L)
¾ cup (150 g) Chinese cabbage, chopped
¾ cup (100 g) carrots, peeled and chopped
¾ cup (100g) white radish, chopped
9 cups (2 L) water
Pinch of salt

Place the vegetables in the water in a stockpot and bring to a boil, then lower the heat and simmer for about an hour until the stock has reduced by about half. Strain and discard the vegetables. This stock will keep for two weeks in a sealed container in the refrigerator.

Steamed vegetable and fish dipping sauce
pla nung jeew
A typical Isan dipping sauce to serve with many kinds of fresh fish and steamed vegetables.

Makes scant ½ cup (100ml)
1 large red chile
2 small red chiles
3 garlic cloves, unpeeled
2 shallots, unpeeled
3 cherry tomatoes
1½ tablespoons fish sauce
1 tablespoon fresh lime juice

Broil the chiles, garlic, shallots, and cherry tomatoes for 10 minutes, until brown. Let cool. When cool enough to handle, peel off the skins, and, using a mortar and pestle, pound them to a fine paste. Add the fish sauce and lime juice, mix well, and set aside to cool—the sauce is served cool, because reheating it makes the lime taste bitter.

Chili sauce
sriracha sauce
This famous sauce from Sriracha is loved in Asia for its unique flavor, which goes perfectly with things like omelets, fried oysters, seafood, and meatballs.

Makes scant ½ cup (100 ml)
10 red chiles
10 cloves garlic, peeled
1 tablespoon white vinegar
1 teaspoon salt
1 teaspoon superfine sugar
½ tablespoon water

Blend all the ingredients together in a blender for about 5 minutes until fine. Store in an airtight jar in the refrigerator.

Isan chili sauce
nam jim jeew
One of the most popular sauces of the Isan region, this goes with dishes such as Crying Tiger (see pages 78–79) and grilled pork, chicken, or fish.

Makes scant ½ cup (100 ml)
2 teaspoons chili powder
2 teaspoons ground roasted rice
½ teaspoon superfine sugar
2 tablespoons fresh lime juice
1 tablespoon fish sauce
2 tablespoons light soy sauce
1 teaspoon chopped shallots
1 teaspoon chopped cilantro

Mix the chili powder, ground roasted rice, sugar, lime juice, fish sauce, and light soy sauce in a bowl until the sugar has dissolved. Sprinkle on the shallots and cilantro and serve.

Breakfast delivery in Chiang Mai—rice is mashed and grilled to make rice wafers.

Satay sauce

nam jim satay

This crunchy sweet sauce is especially made to go with satays and steamed vegetables or salad.

Makes 1¾ cups (400 ml)
1¾ cups (400 ml) Coconut Milk (see page 16)
½ tablespoon Red Curry Paste (see page 15)
1 cup (125 g) roasted peanuts, coarsely ground
5 tablespoons superfine sugar
1 teaspoon salt

Heat the coconut milk in a saucepan and add the curry paste, stirring until the oil separates and rises to the surface. Add the ground peanuts and stir until the paste thickens, then add the sugar and salt and serve.

Seafood sauce

nam jim thalay

Delicious with all seafood including dishes of mussels, grilled shrimp, and fresh crab.

Makes scant ½ cup (100 ml)
4 garlic cloves, peeled
4 small red chiles
2 cilantro roots
Small pinch of sea salt
1 teaspoon sugar
3 tablespoons fresh lime juice
2 tablespoons fish sauce
1 tablespoon chopped cilantro

Using a mortar and pestle, pound the garlic, chiles, cilantro roots, and sea salt together.

Combine the sugar, lime juice, and fish sauce in a bowl, stirring until the sugar dissolves. Add the pounded paste and mix well, then sprinkle in the chopped cilantro.

Chicken sauce

This is the sauce to serve with grilled and deep-fried chicken and with appetizers such as fishcakes.

Makes scant ½ cup (100 ml)
3 tablespoons water
½ cup (100 g) superfine sugar
3 tablespoons white wine vinegar
1 long red chile, chopped
2 pickled garlic cloves, chopped
1 teaspoon salt
1 tablespoon fish sauce

Boil the water with the sugar in a small saucepan, stirring until the sugar dissolves, then add the vinegar. Remove from the heat.

Blend the chile and pickled garlic until fine and add to the ingredients in the saucepan. Stir together over low heat until the sauce thickens. Add the salt and fish sauce and serve.

Fish sauce with chiles

prik nam pla

Every Thai household has its own way of making this flavorful chili sauce. It's a real favorite, which we love to add to rice.

Makes scant ¼ cup (40 ml)
2 chiles, chopped
1½ tablespoons fish sauce
1 teaspoon fresh lime juice

Simply combine the ingredients in a bowl and stir.

Cucumber relish

arjar

This is a delicious accompaniment for all strong curries, including mussaman, venison, and lamb, and it also goes well with chicken satays. You can keep this relish in an airtight, sterilized jar (see page 14) in the refrigerator for a couple of months, adding the freshly chopped ingredients to serve.

Makes 2 cups (450 ml)
1 cup (225 ml) water
½ cup (100 g) superfine sugar
½ cup (125 ml) white wine vinegar
Pinch of salt
1 cucumber, sliced, then the slices quartered
1 shallot, finely sliced
2 small red chiles, finely chopped
4 cilantro leaves, to garnish

Boil the water in a small saucepan and add the sugar, stirring until it dissolves. Add the vinegar and salt and remove from the heat. Let the mixture cool.

Serve the relish in a small dish or bowl, adding the slices of cucumber, shallot, and chiles. Garnish with the cilantro leaves.

Chili vinegar

nam som prik dong

Usually served with Thai noodles in both soups and stir-fried noodle dishes. The chile can be chopped or left whole, and you can make a larger quantity to store in a jar ready for use.

Makes 3 tablespoons (35 ml)
2 chiles, chopped
2 tablespoons vinegar

Combine the chiles and vinegar.

Making crispy-fried shrimp cakes with curry powder and curry leaves.

Index

25 Super Cool
Math Board Games

Easy-To-Play Reproducible Games That Teach Essential Math Skills

By Lorraine Hopping Egan

New York ✳ Toronto ✳ London ✳ Auckland ✳ Sydney
✳ Mexico City ✳ New Delhi ✳ Hong Kong ✳

Acknowledgments

The author would like to thank Chris and Louise for playing
so hard and all of her former math teachers for making her work so hard.

❄ ❄ ❄

Teachers may photocopy the designated reproducible pages for classroom use. No other
part of this publication may be reproduced in whole or in part, or stored in a retrieval system,
or transmitted in any form or by any means, electronic, mechanical, photocopying or otherwise, without written permission of the publisher. For information regarding permission write to
Scholastic Inc., 555 Broadway, New York, NY 10012.

❄ ❄ ❄

Cover design by Pamela Simmons
Cover art by Teresa Anderko
Interior Illustration by Teresa Anderko
Interior design by Pamela Simmons

❄ ❄ ❄

ISBN: 0-590-37872-4
Copyright © 1999 by Lorraine Hopping Egan. All rights reserved.
Printed in the U.S.A.

Table of Contents

Classroom Strategies for Using Board Games

The 25 math board games in this book motivate students to practice a variety of math skills, from basic computation to logical thinking. The games are easy to assemble, fast to play (most take less than 15 minutes), and often addictive! Here's an overview to help you choose the games that best suit your classroom needs:

● **Skill Levels:** The games in each section are generally ordered from easiest to hardest, though variations in the rules provide flexibility in skill levels. All 25 games include at least one skill challenge to encourage players to extend their math skills. Many games include rules or versions for multi-level play. For example, Skyscraper Run-Up includes five games in one, each of which is tougher than the last. Players can play Skeleton Key on any one of three levels of play. The arithmetic game Gopher Golf is a simpler version of Mole Holes. The geometry game Peachy Keen is a more challenging version of Snake Pit.

● **Skill Versus Luck:** Most games require a mix of strategy and luck so that students of different ability levels can play competitively together. These games rely on skill alone: Wolves and Coyotes, Number Island, The Eliminators, Factor Bowling, Mole Holes, Decimal Dare, Linkopolis, Snake Pit, Peachy Keen, Daisy Chain, and Triplets. After the first session of a game, encourage players to share their winning strategies with the class.

● **Cooperative Play:** These games can be played cooperatively: The Eliminators (have students work in teams of two or three to find the target number), Number Island, Mole Holes, Decimal Dare, and Happy Go Logic.

● **Number of Players:** The majority of the games are designed for the standard two to four players. Usually, playing with more than four players results in too much "downtime" between turns.

These games are appropriate for the entire class to play at once: Skyscraper Run-Up, The Eliminators, What's for Lunch?, and Decimal Dare.

Solitaire rules are provided for these games: Skyscraper Run-Up, Number Island, Factor Bowling, Mole Holes, Snake Pit, Peachy Keen, Booby Trap!, Probability on Ice (beat your best score), Happy Go Logic (beat the Jester), and Triplets.

Deciding Who Goes First

Before every game, players will have to decide fairly who takes the first turn. Game play always goes clockwise (to the first player's left). Besides the traditional coin flip or picking a number from 1 to 10, here are three fair methods of choosing who goes first:

● **Two Players:** One player holds a counter in either hand behind his or her back. The opponent picks the player's right or left hand. If that hand contains the counter, the opponent goes first. Otherwise, the player holding the counter goes first.

● **Two Players:** Play several rounds of "Paper, Scissors, Rock." At the same time, each player forms paper (a flat hand), scissors (a peace sign), or rock (a fist) out of one hand. Paper beats rock; rock beats scissors; scissors beats paper. The first player to win two rounds goes first.

● **Two or More Players:** Place a random number of counters (15 to 20) in the middle of the table. Starting with the player whose birthdate is last on the calendar and continuing clockwise, each player takes either one or two counters in turn. The last player to take a counter goes first.

Finding Place Markers

Place markers are playing pieces that mark a player's place on the board. Each player needs a distinctly unique place marker that's smaller than the spaces on the board but that can be easily picked up.

Suggestions include bottle caps, small binder clips, chess pieces, empty film canisters, erasers, egg carton cups (cut them apart and turn them upside down; color or decorate them to make them distinct), stones, chestnuts or shelled peanuts (color or decorate them), and leftover playing pieces from old board games.

Finding Counters

Counters help players keep score. They either mark captured positions on the board or players trade and earn them during the game. Usually, counters should be small and uniform. Sometimes, players need distinct counters—one player uses dried lima beans and another uses dried chick peas, for example.

Suggestions include dried beans, dried pasta (dye it to make distinct counters), beads, buttons, tiddly winks, craft sticks, checkers, backgammon pieces, colorful label dots (cut them apart, but don't peel them off), small poker chips, toothpicks (especially colored ones), washers, nuts and bolts, pebbles, large pieces of aquarium gravel, paper clips and similar small office supplies, and bobby pins or hairpins.

Making and Using Spinners

The Fast and Easy Way: To make a pointer, unbend the end of a large paper clip. Place the round end of the clip over the center of the spinner. Place a pencil on the center point. Spin the paper clip around the pencil. The clip must make at least two full rotations; otherwise, the player must spin again.

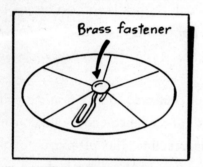

The Sturdy Way

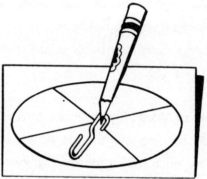

The Fast and Easy Way

The Sturdy Way: To make a pointer, unbend the end of a large paper clip. Photocopy or mount the spinner pattern onto sturdy tag board or cardboard. Laminate the spinner for durability.

Using the end of the paper clip, punch a hole in the center. Place the round end of the clip over the hole. Insert a brass fastener down through the hole and bend the ends flat on the backside to hold the paper clip in place.

Make sure the clip can spin freely. If it sticks or scrapes, loosen the brass fastener. If the clip pops loose, tighten the brass fastener or use a larger one.

The Best Way: Cut out and mount the spinner pattern onto a commercial spinner from an old board game. Sturdy spinners with plastic pointers give more reliable results than homemade spinners. Look for them at scrap material stores and garage sales.

GAME

1 # Wolves and Coyotes

Players: 2

Players spread their predators around Rational Park and take over each other's territories.

SKILLS Inequalities of whole numbers, addition and subtraction, problem-solving strategies

PREPARATION The two Rational Park boards (pages 10, 11) provide number practice on two levels of play. Choose the board suitable for your students, and make one copy for each pair. Make one copy of the rules (page 8) for each player.

Provide each pair with two different kinds of small, flat counters. For Smelly Mountain, each pair will need 72 counters (to represent 36 wolves and 36 coyotes). For Mellowstone, pass out 100 counters (to represent 50 wolves and 50 coyotes) per pair.

Basic Math Skills

Whole number inequalities can be as simple as the card game War—the higher number always wins. In Wolves and Coyotes, players decide where to place higher and lower numbers of predators to protect territories from takeover by other predators.

Each territory must have at least one animal. How many territories are in the park? (12 for Smelly Mountain; 20 for Mellowstone) How many territories does each predator start with? (6 and 10, respectively) What's the greatest number of animals one territory can hold? (Smelly Mountain: 36 territories − 5 one-animal territories = 31 animals in one territory; Mellowstone: 50 − 9 = 41.) What is the average number of animals per territory? ($36 \div 6 = 6$ in Smelly Mountain; $50 \div 5 = 10$ in Mellowstone)

Is it wise to divide animals equally among the territories? Why or why not? After students play the game, discuss other strategies.

Skill Challenge

● Use the Mellowstone Rational Park board to play a geometry and logic game called Picasso. Two to three players each have a different-colored pen or marker. The first player colors any territory on the board. Players then take turns coloring in territories. Here's the hitch: They can't color two adjacent territories the same color. The goal is to be the last player to make a legal play.

Wolves and Coyotes

Players: 2

SKILLS Inequalities of whole numbers, addition and subtraction, problem–solving strategies

MATERIALS
- Rational Park game board
- 36 or 50 counters for wolves and 36 or 50 counters for coyotes

Playing the Game

One player leads a pack of wolves; the other leads the coyotes. Spread your predators around Rational Park. Then try to take over one another's territories by using greater numbers of predators against lesser numbers.

1. Each player picks either wolves or coyotes. The number of predators you have depends on the park you are in:

   Smelly Mountain Rational Park: 36 predators per player

   Mellowstone Rational Park: 50 predators per player

2. The wolves enter the park first. Pick any territory and place some wolves there. The exact number is up to you, but each territory must have at least one animal. You can't change your mind, so choose the number wisely.

3. The coyotes enter the park next. Pick a territory and place coyotes there.

4. Take turns placing predators in the park until both players have placed all of their animals. You may end up with too few animals (leaving a territory empty). If so, your opponent can move one of your predators from any territory to the empty territory in order to correct your mistake.

Wolves and Coyotes

Players: 2

5. The goal is to take over your opponent's territories. Follow these park rules:

- The coyotes make the first takeover. Then players take turns.

- A territory with greater numbers can take over a territory with lesser numbers as long as the territories share a border.

- You can take only one territory per turn.

- Add the numbers in two of your territories for a more powerful takeover. Each of your territories must share a border with the territory you are taking over.

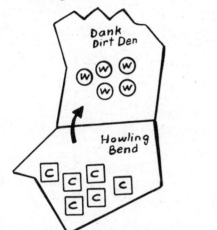

A territory with 6 coyotes can take over a territory with 5 wolves.

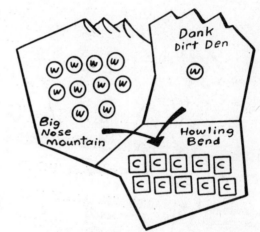

Territories with 10 wolves and 1 wolf combine to take over a territory with 10 coyotes.

6. To take over a territory, remove the other player's animals. Move any number of your animals into the new territory. The animals must come from the attacking territory (or territories). Always leave at least one animal in each territory.

7. The game ends when neither predator can make a play. The winner is the predator with the most territories. The number of animals in the park doesn't count toward winning or losing.

MATH STRATEGY TIP When placing animals, think about how many borders a territory has. Territories with lots of borders are powerful because they can take over several areas—but they are also more open to attack.

Wolves and Coyotes

Game Board

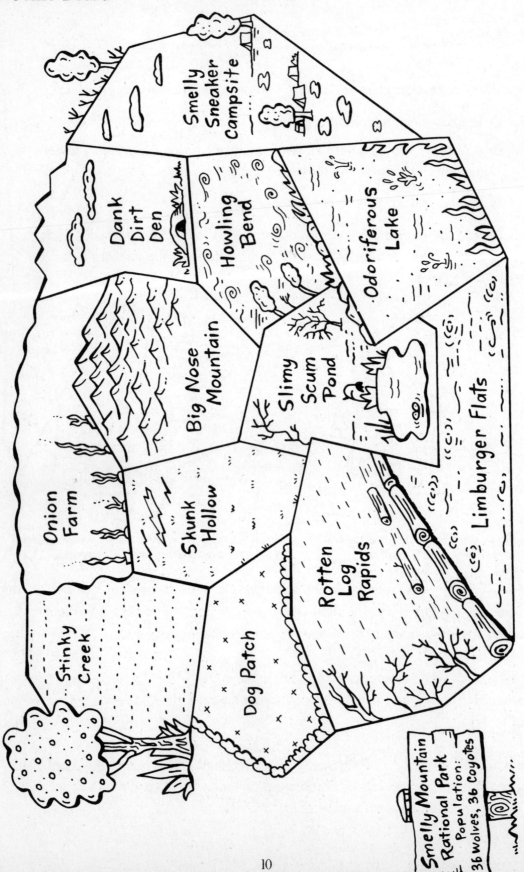

Smelly Sneaker Campsite

Dank Dirt Den

Howling Bend

Odoriferous Lake

Big Nose Mountain

Slimy Scum Pond

Limburger Flats

Onion Farm

Skunk Hollow

Rotten Log Rapids

Stinky Creek

Dog Patch

Smelly Mountain Rational Park: Population: 36 Wolves, 36 Coyotes

Wolves and Coyotes

Game Board

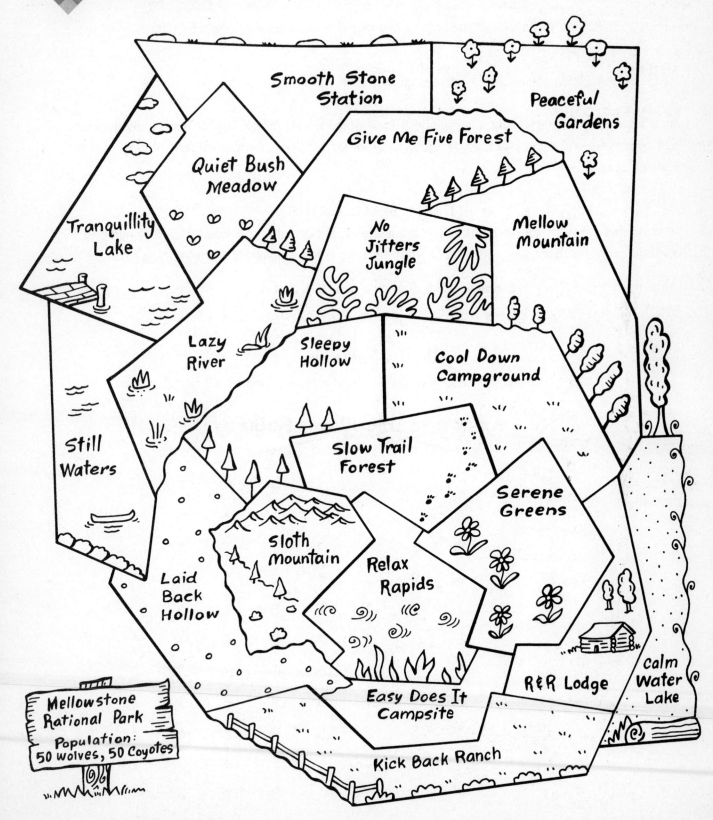

Smooth Stone Station

Peaceful Gardens

Give Me Five Forest

Quiet Bush Meadow

Tranquillity Lake

No Jitters Jungle

Mellow Mountain

Lazy River

Sleepy Hollow

Cool Down Campground

Still Waters

Slow Trail Forest

Serene Greens

Sloth Mountain

Laid Back Hollow

Relax Rapids

Easy Does It Campsite

R&R Lodge

Calm Water Lake

Mellowstone Rational Park
Population: 50 wolves, 50 Coyotes

Kick Back Ranch

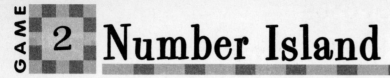

2 Number Island

Players claim islands by circling two or more numbers that add up to 10.

SKILLS
Addition of one-digit numbers, mental math

PREPARATION
Photocopy one Number Island game board (page 14) for each individual or pair of players and a copy of the rules (page 13) for each player. Give each pair of players two markers of a different color.

Basic Math Skills

Share this simple mental math trick with the students: When adding a long column of numbers, combine numbers that add up to 10 first. Then add the leftover numbers to the running total.

Example: 7 + 4 + 6 + 5 + 3 + 5 + 1 = ?

A quick glance reveals that (4 + 6) + (7 + 3) + (5 + 5) + 1 = 31.

Skill Challenge

● Have students choose a higher target number, such as 12 or 15.

Answer to One-Player Rules

Answers may vary. Possible answer:

Number Island

Players: 1 or 2

SKILLS   Addition of one-digit numbers, mental math

MATERIALS
- Number Island game board
- 2 markers of different colors (one per player)

Playing the Game

Number Island has plenty of land up for grabs. Find it—and claim it—by circling numbers that add up to 10.

1. To take a turn, circle two or more neighboring numbers that add up to 10. Follow these rules:

- The numbers must be side-by-side, up-and-down, or diagonal.
- Once a number is circled, it is out of play for the rest of the game.
- You can't circle a number that has already been claimed.

side-by-side	up-and-down	diagonal	combination

5 3 2	6
	 4
		1
		    9
			3 5
			      2

2. Players take turns circling numbers that add up to 10. The game ends when no more plays are left.

3. Players score one point for each circle (not for each number in a circle). The winner is the player with the most circles.

ONE-PLAYER RULES   Try to claim every number on the board. It's not easy!

MATH STRATEGY TIP   Make a list of two-and three-number combinations that add up to 10.

Number Island

Game Board

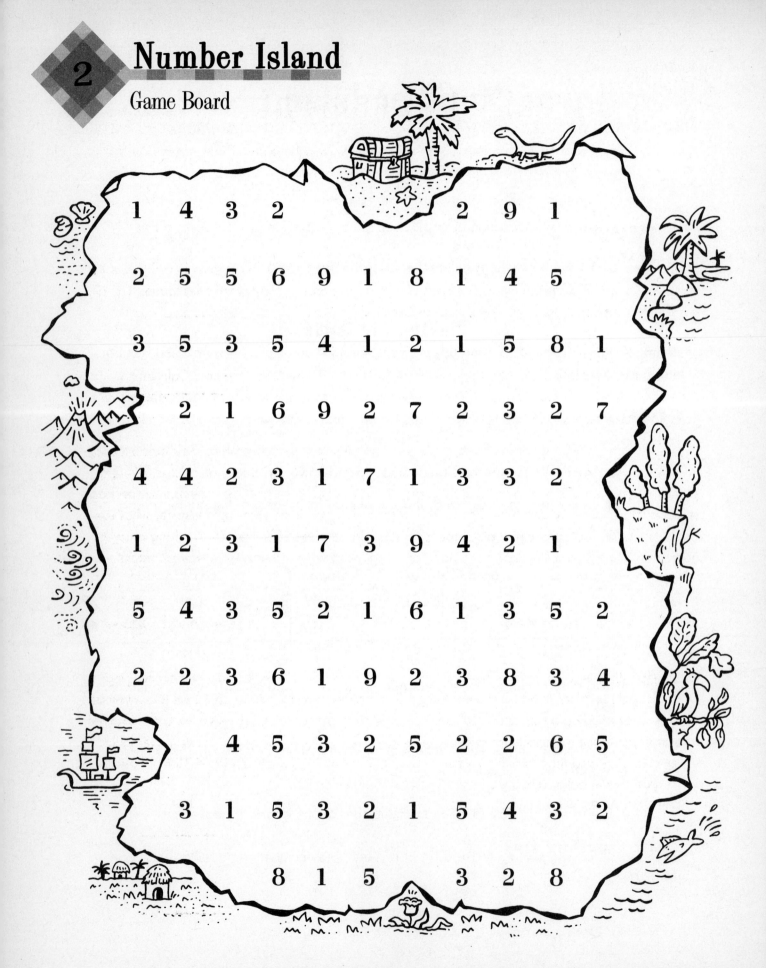

3 Bargain Chasement

Players: 2 to 4

Race around the Bargain Chasement, snatching up bargains. The winner is the first player to buy $1,000 (or more) worth of merchandise.

SKILLS Addition and subtraction of whole numbers, multiplication and division, money

PREPARATION Provide each group of players with a Bargain Chasement game board (page 19), a spinner (page 18), a place marker for each player, scrap paper, a copy of the rules (pages 16–17), a calculator (optional; for double-checking answers).

Basic Math Skills

For most of us, shopping accounts for much of the every day math that we use. Calculating or estimating discounts in our heads is something we learn to do automatically as we compare one product with another.

Although Bargain Chasement allows players to use paper and pencil to make their calculations, have them use the following methods to practice estimating amounts mentally as a class. Move a place marker from one item on the game board to the next. At each item, spin the spinner and ask students to call out a "ballpark figure" for the discounted price of the item. For instance, what's about half of $114? Students might respond: $50, $70, or even $57. There's no wrong answer here. The idea is to get students in the habit of recognizing when an answer is way off track.

Skill Challenges

● Tell students to change the dollar amounts of items to include cents. To ensure round numbers, all amounts must be evenly divisible by 6 (i.e., divisible by both 2 and 3).

● Change the bargains on the Bargain Chasement spinner to more mathematically challenging deals such as $19.99 off (shortcut: subtract $20 and then add a penny), 50% off (the same as half off or dividing by 2), and 10% off. For 10% off, players can either move the decimal point one place to the left and then subtract ($114.00 − $11.40 = $102.60) or multiply the dollar amount by 9 and then divide the answer by 10 ($114 x 9 = 1,026; 1,026 ÷ 10 = $102.60) or multiply the dollar amount by 0.9 ($114 x 0.9 = $102.60).

Bargain Chasement

Players: 2 to 4

SKILLS Addition and subtraction of whole numbers, multiplication and division, money

MATERIALS
- Bargain Chasement game board
- Bargain Chasement spinner
- 2 to 4 place markers
- scrap paper (to keep a running total of scores)
- calculator (optional)

Playing the Game

Who can spend $1,000 (or more) at the Bargain Chasement store?

1. Place all place markers on the space labeled "START SPENDING!" Each player records a starting score of $25 and then moves a number of spaces equal to the month of his or her birthday (1 space for January, 2 spaces for February, and so on).

2. To take a turn, spin the spinner. Apply the bargain on the spinner to the dollar amount on the space where your place marker is.

Examples:

Dollar Amount	Bargain	You spend
$150 kettle drum	Take $\frac{1}{2}$ off.	$150 – ($150÷2) = $75
$192 electric guitar	Take $15 off.	$192 – $15 = $177
$114 movie pass	Take $\frac{1}{3}$ off.	$114 – ($114÷3) = $76

3. Add the amount you spent (not the original price of the item!) to your score. Keep a running total. Use a calculator only to double-check your answers. The penalty for a math mistake is to subtract $100 from your running total.

4. To begin each new turn, look at the number in the ones (one dollar) place of your current total. Move that many spaces. (*A 0 means that you must stay where you are.*)

Example: Your total is $273. Move 3 spaces.

5. If you land on "All Shopped Out!", wait a turn. Then move forward 1 space.

Bargain Chasement

Players: 2 to 4

6. Every time you land on or pass START SPENDING!, buy a $25 gift certificate. (Add $25 to your total.)

7. The first player to spend $1,000 or more is the winner.

MATH STRATEGY TIP   Look for math shortcuts when taking discounts. To take half off, divide the total by 2. To take one-third off, divide the total by 3.

Bargain Chasement Place Markers

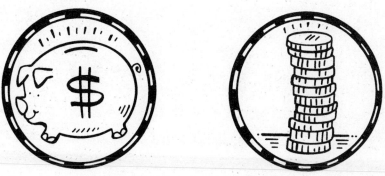

Bargain Chasement

Spinner

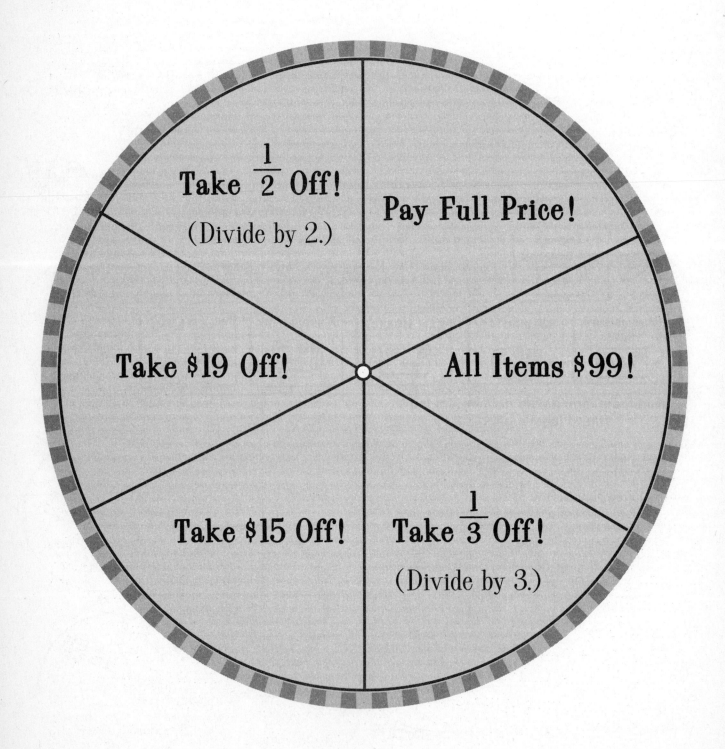

Take $\frac{1}{2}$ Off!
(Divide by 2.)

Pay Full Price!

Take $19 Off!

All Items $99!

Take $15 Off!

Take $\frac{1}{3}$ Off!
(Divide by 3.)

3

Bargain Chasement

Game Board

Free Helicopter Ride Back to START

Flea Circus $132

Prairie Dog Village $84

Pets You Won't Regret

Camel Cab $138

Cheap Thrills and Frills

Merry-Go-Round Horse $156

Leaning Tower of Pizza $258

Admit 1 ★ FOREVER!

Lifetime Movie Pass $114

Dance Lessons $96

Yellow Bellows $138

ALL SHOPPED OUT! Wait here 1 turn. Then move 1 space.

Anvil Paperweight $222

Ye Olde Tool Shedde

Platinum Pliers $102

START $25.00 GIFT CERTIFICATE SPENDING

Hear the Music Department

Kettle Drum $150

Golden Horn $120

Electric Guitar $192

GAME

4 The Eliminators

2 or more individuals or pairs,
plus The Boss (the game monitor)

The Boss orders secret agents to eliminate a series of numbers on a number chart; for example, The Boss might say, "Eliminate all numbers that are evenly divisible by 3." To win, players zero in on the correct target number—the last remaining number on the chart.

SKILLS Number patterns, computation, factors and multiples, divisibility rules

PREPARATION Provide one copy of the rules for each student (page 21) and two copies of the number chart (page 24) per player or pair of players. (The extra chart is in case students make a mistake and want to start over.) Give each player or pair two or three highlighters or markers of different colors. Choose one of the missions (pages 22–23) based on skill level—from easy to challenging.

Basic Math Skills

The game provides practice in a variety of number skills from identifying even and odd numbers to recognizing number patterns. As a warm-up, play the first game together, using a different color highlighter for each order. Note that some steps eliminate numbers that are already crossed out. Point out number patterns as they become evident—all the numbers with the digit 7 in them are in one row and one column, for example. Review the following divisibility rules with the students:

- Any even number is divisible by 2.
- Add the digits. If the sum is divisible by 3, then the original number is divisible by 3. **Example:** 39: 3 + 9 = 12, which is divisible by 3. If the sum is divisible by 9, then so is the original number. **Example:** 27: 2 + 7 = 9, which is divisible by 9.
- If the last two digits are divisible by 4, then the number is divisible by 4. **Example:** 128: 28 is divisible by 4.
- If the number is divisible by 2 and 3, it is divisible by 6.
- If the number is divisible by 2 and 4, it is divisible by 8.
- Numbers that end in 0 or 5 are divisible by 5; those that end in 0 are divisible by 10.
- Double digits (11, 22, 33, . . .) are divisible by 11.

Skill Challenge

- Challenge students to create their own mission for others to play.

The Eliminators

**Players: 2 or more individuals or
pairs, plus The Boss**

SKILLS Number patterns, computation, factors and multiples, divisibility rules

MATERIALS
- Eliminators Number Chart (one copy per player)
- Mission Orders (for The Boss's eyes only)
- highlighters or markers of different colors

Playing the Game

Follow all orders from The Boss and cross out numbers on the chart. To win, find the target number—the only number left at the end of the mission.

1. The Boss will read a series of orders aloud. Each order will tell you which numbers on the chart to eliminate (cross out) with your highlighters or markers. Listen carefully!

2. When only one number remains, circle the number and raise your hand. (Shhh! Don't give away the answer!) Players who find the correct target number win the game. Only The Boss can tell you if you have won.

MATH STRATEGY TIP Look for patterns in the numbers that you eliminate. For example, numbers evenly divisible by 9 are on a diagonal in the chart. Numbers divisible by 11 are on an opposite diagonal. Math divisibility rules will help you decide what numbers to eliminate.

Math Divisibility Rules

- Any even number is divisible by 2.
- Add the digits. If the sum is divisible by 3, then the original number is divisible by 3. **Example:** 39: 3 + 9 = 12, which is divisible by 3. If the sum is divisible by 9, then so is the original number. **Example:** 27: 2 + 7 = 9, which is divisible by 9.
- If the last two digits are divisible by 4, then the number is divisible by 4. **Example:** 128: 28 is divisible by 4.
- If the number is divisible by 2 and 3, it is divisible by 6.
- If the number is divisible by 2 and 4, it is divisible by 8.
- Numbers that end in 0 or 5 are divisible by 5; those that end in 0 are divisible by 10.
- Double digits (11, 22, 33, . . .) are divisible by 11.

4 The Eliminators

The Boss's Orders

Mission 1 Orders *(easy)*

1. Eliminate all numbers that have the digit 7 in them.

2. Eliminate all numbers that have the digit 3 in them.

3. Eliminate all the even numbers except 100.

4. Eliminate all numbers that have two digits that are the same.
   [Note to Boss: This includes 100.]

5. Eliminate all numbers that end in 0 or 5. Or eliminate all numbers that can be evenly divided by 5.

6. Of the numbers that remain, eliminate the first 6 numbers in the chart.

7. Eliminate odd numbers greater than 50 but less than 100.

8. Circle the target number. (49)

Mission 2 Orders
(easy to medium)

1. Eliminate all the odd numbers.

2. Starting with 4, count by 4's and eliminate every fourth number (4, 8, 12, and so on). Or eliminate all numbers that are evenly divisible by 4.

3. Eliminate all the numbers that are greater than 22 and less than 68.
   [Note to Boss: This does not include 22 and 68.]

4. Eliminate all the one-digit numbers.

5. Eliminate all the numbers whose digits are not the same (e.g., 14 because 1 and 4 are not the same).

6. Circle the target number. (22)

Mission 3 Orders *(medium)*

1. Eliminate the numbers 1, 2, 3, 5, 8, 13, 21, and 34. [Note to Boss: These are the first numbers in the famous Fibonacci number series.]

2. Eliminate all numbers greater than or equal to 56 AND less than or equal to 78.

3. Eliminate 9 and all of its multiples.

4. Eliminate all numbers with the digits 0, 1, 2, and 3.

5. Eliminate all numbers greater than or equal to 84 OR less than 48.

6. Eliminate the next two numbers in the pattern of numbers in step 1. [Note to Boss: Repeat the numbers in step 1. To continue the series, add the last two numbers: 21 + 34 = 55; 34 + 55 = 89.]

7. Of the numbers left, eliminate the greater number.

8 Circle the target number. (48)

The Eliminators

The Boss's Orders

Mission 4 Orders
(hard)

1. Eliminate all the squares of whole numbers, including 1 (1 x 1), 4 (2 x 2), 9 (3 x 3) and so on.

2. Eliminate numbers that fit this pattern (including the numbers given): 1, 3, 6, 10, 15, 21, and so on. [Note to Boss: Add 2, add 3, add 4, and so on.]

3. Eliminate numbers that fit this pattern (including the numbers given): 5, 14, 23, 32, 41, and so on. [Note to Boss: Starting with 5, add 9.]

4. Eliminate numbers greater than 60 OR less than 30.

5. Eliminate numbers whose digits add up to an even number.

6. Eliminate numbers that ARE NOT evenly divisible by 10.

7. Circle the target number. (30)

Mission 5 Orders
(super challenge)

1. Eliminate 100 and all of its factors.

2. Eliminate 3 and all of its multiples.

3. Eliminate 7 and all of its multiples.

4. Eliminate all of the prime numbers.

5. Eliminate 8 and all of its multiples AND any number with an 8 as a digit.

6. Eliminate all numbers evenly divisible by 11 OR 13.

7. Eliminate all numbers greater than or equal to 62.

8. Eliminate all numbers evenly divisible by 17.

9. Circle the target number. (46)

23

The Eliminators

4

Secret Agent's Name _____

1	2	3	4	5	6	7	8	9	10
11	12	13	14	15	16	17	18	19	20
21	22	23	24	25	26	27	28	29	30
31	32	33	34	35	36	37	38	39	40
41	42	43	44	45	46	47	48	49	50
51	52	53	54	55	56	57	58	59	60
61	62	63	64	65	66	67	68	69	70
71	72	73	74	75	76	77	78	79	80
81	82	83	84	85	86	87	88	89	90
91	92	93	94	95	96	97	98	99	100

Remainder Raccoon

Players: 2 to 4

Players are hungry raccoons, racing through the spoils of a human picnic. To earn their dinner, they must spin a number, divide a larger number on the board by that number, and find the remainder.

SKILLS Division with remainders

PREPARATION Cut out the raccoon place markers at the bottom of this page (one per player) and laminate them. Provide each playing group with a Remainder Raccoon game board (page 28), a spinner (page 27), a copy of the rules (page 26), and scrap paper.

Basic Math Skills

The division problems in Remainder Raccoon generate remainders. The higher the remainder, the faster the player-raccoon speeds through the picnic. (A remainder of 0 means the raccoon is stuck in place until the next turn.)

Ask the students to analyze the numbers on the game board. Which numbers will produce a lot of remainders, and why? (Prime numbers have no factors other than 1 and themselves, and so will generate a remainder for each number on the spinner.) Which numbers will be toughest to advance on? (Numbers that are multiples of several divisors, such as those at the end of the game.)

Group players by math ability.

Skill Challenge

● Urge students to create a Raccoon Remainder game with three- and four-digit numbers. They can place prime numbers toward the beginning and multiples toward the end.

Raccoon Place Markers

Remainder Raccoon

Players: 2 to 4

SKILLS Division with remainders

MATERIALS
- Remainder Raccoon game board
- Remainder Raccoon spinner
- 2 to 4 raccoon place markers
- scrap paper

Playing the Game

You're a hungry raccoon! Divide to find the remainders (leftovers) of a human picnic. The higher the remainder, the faster you finish.

1. Place all raccoons on "Start."

2. To take a turn, spin the spinner. Divide the number on the first space by the number on the spinner. Announce the division sentence aloud. All players should do the division sentence and compare answers.

Example: You spin 4. The number on the first space is 37. Announce the division sentence: "37 ÷ 4." All players calculate to find the answer of 18 with a remainder of 1 (18 R1).

Move your raccoon the same number of spaces as the remainder—not the number of the answer. In the example, you would move 1 space. Your turn ends.

3. Take turns spinning and moving until a lucky raccoon reaches the den and wins. The winner does not need an exact number to enter the den.

MATH STRATEGY TIP Look for shortcuts. For example, all odd numbers divided by 2 always leave a remainder of 1. For numbers divided by 5 or 10, count by fives or tens up to the number. The remainder is the number left over. For 31 ÷ 5, count 10, 15, 20, 25, 30; there's 1 left over. For 93 ÷ 10, count by tens up to 90. There are 3 left over.

5

Remainder Raccoon

Spinner

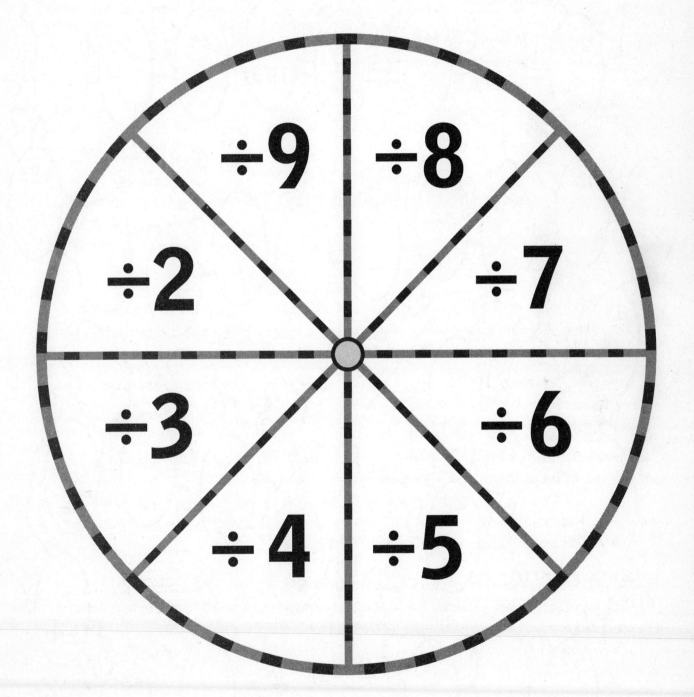

Remainder Raccoon

Game Board

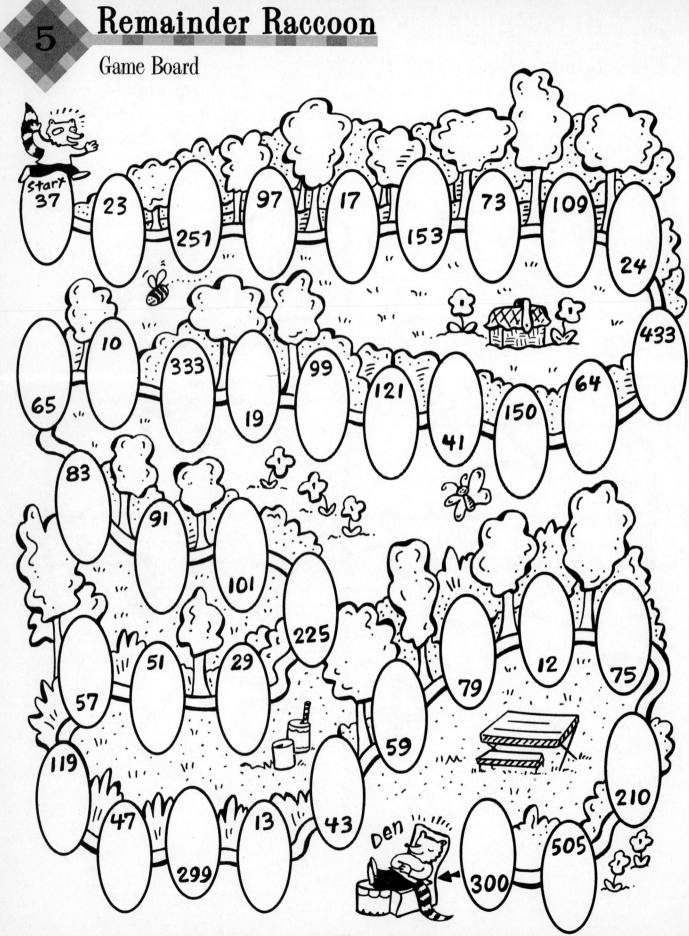

6 Skeleton Key

Players follow one of three paths (easy, medium, or hard) through a haunted house. To open a door, a player must have a skeleton key that's a factor of the number on the door (for example, key 4 opens door 12).

SKILLS Factors and multiples

PREPARATION Photocopy the Skeleton Keys (page 31) on opaque tag board and then cut out and laminate them. Provide each playing group with a set of keys, a cup or a bag to hold the keys, a copy of the Skeleton Key game board (page 32), a copy of the rules (page 30), and a place marker for each player.

Basic Math Skills

Skeleton Key provides practice in factors on three levels of play. Multilevel play allows a less skilled player to play competitively (on level 1) against a more skilled player (who plays simultaneously on level 2 or 3).

To practice finding factors, play a quick game. Divide the class into two teams. Write the numbers 1 through 29 on the board. Each team takes turns choosing a number (a number that is not prime) from the board and finding its factors. For instance, suppose a team chooses the number 28. The team writes all of the factors on the board and adds them: $1 + 2 + 4 + 7 + 14 + 28 = 56$. The score is 56. Play continues until there are only prime numbers left on the board. The winner is the team with the higher score.

What strategies do students discover after playing Skeleton Key? Suppose both keys will open a door: the 2 key and the 3 key both open door 6. Does it matter which key students use? (The 2 key is the better choice since the player can use the 3 key on the next space, which is number 9.) Encourage students to plot their moves one turn in advance.

Skill Challenge

● Add skeleton keys 7, 9, and 10 to the keys included in the game. Duplicate keys 2, 3, and 4 so that there are two of each of these keys.

Skeleton Key

Players: 2 or 3

SKILLS Factors and multiples

MATERIALS
- Skeleton Key game board
- 8 numbered Skeleton Keys (1, 1, 2, 3, 4, 5, 6, and 8)
- cup or bag to hold the keys
- 2 or 3 place markers (one for each player)

Playing the Game

Who can reach the roof of the haunted house first? Choose a path—1, 2, or 3 (if you dare). Then use Skeleton Keys to open doors along the way.

1. Put your place marker on the first number of your chosen path. Put all the keys in a cup or bag. Each player draws a key and keeps it. The player with the highest key goes first.

2. To take a turn, draw a key. (No fair peeking at the numbers before you draw!) Look at the number on the door that your place marker is on. Is either of your two keys a factor of that number? If so, you can use a key "to open the door." To use a key, simply put it back in the bag or cup. Move your place marker to the next space and end your turn.

- If both keys are factors, you get to choose which one to use.

- If neither key is a factor, discard one key. Wait for your next turn.

3. Players take turns drawing, using, or discarding keys. A player might make a mistake and try to use a key that isn't a factor. If this happens, the player must discard the key and go back 1 space.

4. The winner is the player who reaches the roof—the prime number 101—and uses the 1 key to open the final door.

MATH STRATEGY TIP The 1 key can open any door, but it is the only key that can open the last door. Use it wisely. Also, pay attention to which key your opponent needs. You can block his or her play by holding onto a "key" number.

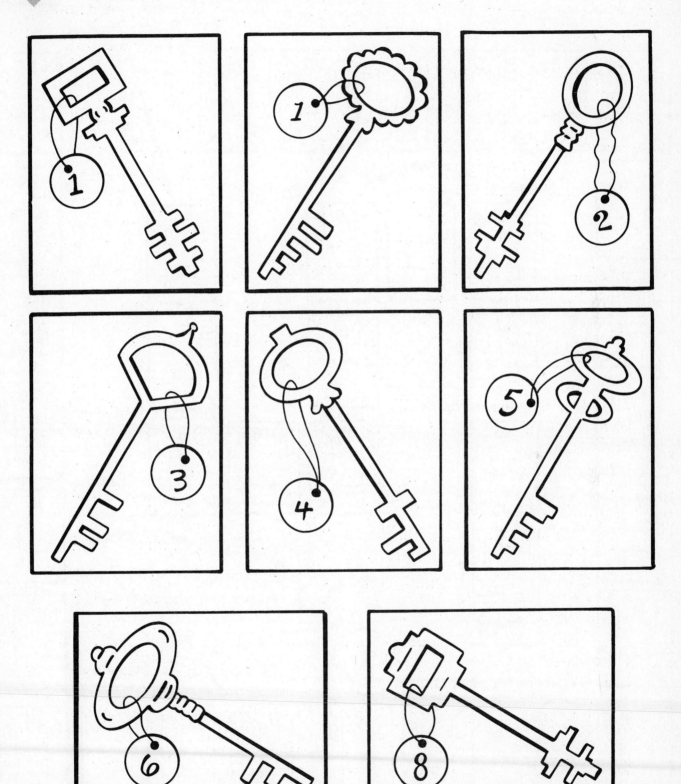

6

Skeleton Key

Game Board

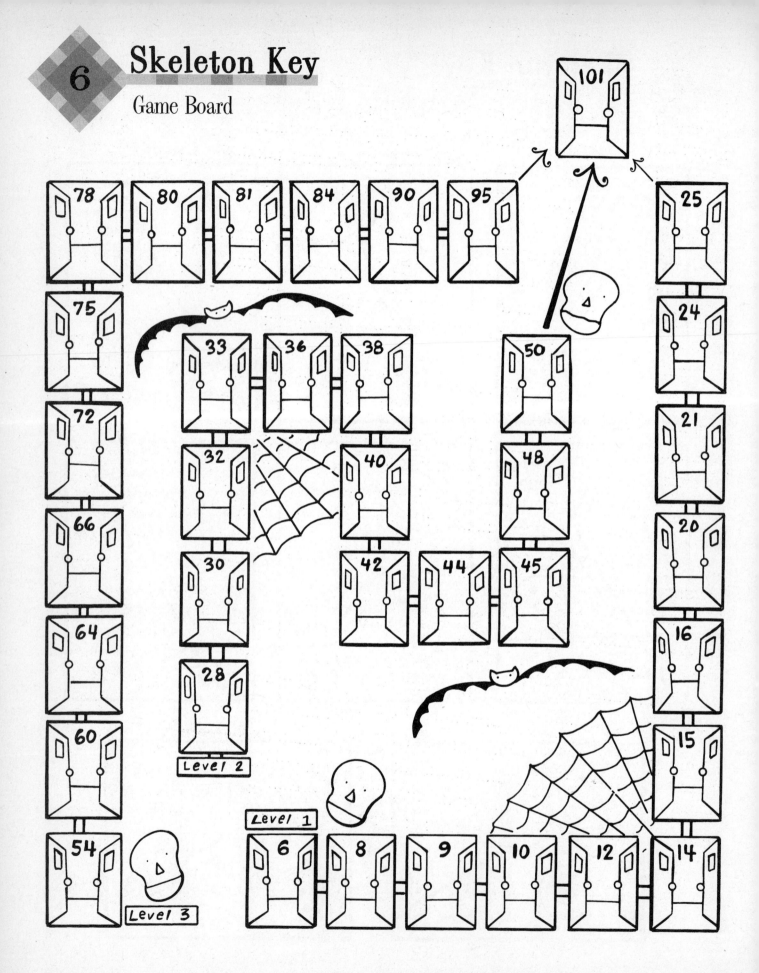

GAME 7 | Factor Bowling

Players: 1 or 2

One player knocks down multiples while the other knocks down factors.

SKILLS Factors and multiples

PREPARATION Provide each pair of players with one copy per game of the Factor Bowling game board (page 36), a copy of the rules (pages 34–35), and two markers of different colors.

Basic Math Skills

After playing Factor Bowling, students will be able to mentally identify factors and multiples from 2 to 50. To practice mentally figuring multiples before playing the game, count by 2's, by 3's, by 4's, and so on up to 12's. To practice factors, see the Tax Collector game described in the Basic Math Skills section of the previous game, Skeleton Key (page 29).

After students play Factor Bowling from both points of view (multiples and factors), discuss strategies for winning. For example, if a player owns Multiple Alley, which numbers make good first choices to circle? (In general, choose a number that eliminates more of your opponent's numbers than your own numbers. Numbers such as 28 have lots of lesser factors—2, 4, 7, 14—but no large factor on the board.) Which numbers are poor choices? (The number 25, for example, would yield only one factor—5.)

For the player who owns Factor Alley, what are good number choices to start? For each number that students suggest, calculate the net gain (opponent cross-outs minus your own cross-outs). For example, 10 eliminates your own number 20, but also rules out three of your opponent's numbers—30, 40, 50. The net gain is 2. Choosing 11 doesn't rule out any of your own numbers and yields two multiples—33 and 44. Again, the net gain is 2. A bold strategy is to choose the number 2 early, if you can, since the multiples board has more even numbers by a margin of 14 to 9. The net gain is 5.

For the one-player game, the object is to cross out as few numbers as possible for every number circled. Circling these numbers in order produces a net score of 20 (40 points for circled numbers minus 20 points for cross-outs): 46, 21, 25, 18, 50, 20, 35, 14, 34, 19, 26, 16, 39, 12, 27, 8, 45, 4, 33, 6. Many other winning combinations are possible.

Skill Challenge

● Encourage students to create games with greater number sets—24 to 100, for example.

Factor Bowling

Players: 1 or 2

SKILLS Factors and multiples

MATERIALS
- Factor Bowling game board (one copy per game)
- 2 markers of different colors

Playing the Game

Who can knock down the most pins using factors and multiples?

1. One player owns Factor Alley. The other owns Multiple Alley. The Multiple Alley owner goes first.

2. If you are the Multiple Alley owner, here is how to take a turn: Circle any one number in either of your two alleys. Cross out all factors of the circled number in all four alleys (including your two alleys).

    Example: You circle 48 in Multiple Alley. Cross out 24, 12, 8, 4, 3, and 2.

3. If you own Factor Alley, here is how to take a turn: Circle any one number in either of your two alleys. Cross out all multiples of the circled numbers in all four alleys.

    Example: You circle 10 in Factor Alley. Cross out 20, 30, 40, and 50.

4. Once a number has been circled, take turns circling and crossing out numbers (if there are any to cross out). Pay attention to the numbers that your opponent crosses out. If he or she misses a number and you catch the mistake, you score 1 bonus point.

5. The game ends when all numbers have been circled or crossed out. Score as follows:

    Add 2 points for each circled number in your two alleys.
    Subtract 1 point for each crossed-out number in your two alleys.

6. The winner is the player with the higher score, including any bonus points earned during game play.

7. Switch alleys and play again!

Factor Bowling

Players: 1 or 2

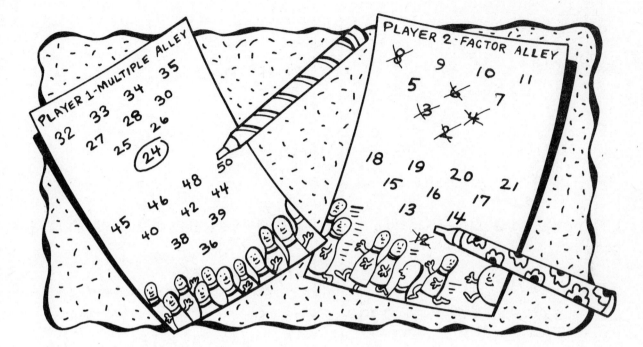

ONE–PLAYER RULES Alternate between circling a number in Multiple Alley and circling a number in Factor Alley. Number each circle in order so that you can retrace your steps later and check for any mistakes. After circling a number, cross out any and all factors and multiples as usual. Remember—once a number has been circled, don't cross it out. After all numbers have been circled or crossed out, score 2 points for each circled number. Subtract 1 point for each crossed-out number. Play again and better your score! A score of 20 is excellent.

MATH STRATEGY TIP Keep in mind the following: The owner of Multiple Alley always crosses out numbers that are lesser than the circled number. The owner of Factor Alley always crosses out numbers that are greater than the circled number.

In the two-player game, the object is to find numbers that create a lot of cross-outs. In the one-player game, the goal is just the opposite—to find numbers that don't create cross-outs.

Factor Bowling

7

Game Board

Player 1: Multiple Alley

32   33   34   35

27   28   30

25   26

24

45   46   48   50

40   42   44

38   39

36

Player 2: Factor Alley

8   9   10   11

5   6   7

3   4

2

18   19   20   21

15   16   17

13   14

12

GAME

8 Skyscraper Run-Up

**1 to 6 or more, plus
a game monitor**

Players compute their way from the ground floor to the roof of a skyscraper.

SKILLS Mixed computation of whole numbers, mental math

PREPARATION Make one copy of a Skyscraper Run-Up board or boards (pages 43–47) and the rules (pages 39–40) for each player. Each of the five game boards works as a separate, short game. Or tape together two or more boards into a towering skyscraper for extended play.

Make a copy of either the easier or harder numbered sneakers (pages 41–42) for each group of players. Cut out the sneakers and fold them in half to hide the number. Place all the folded papers in an opaque bag to use in a blind drawing.

Basic Math Skills

The Skyscraper Run-Up game is a mathematical version of the annual Empire State Building Run-Up race. In this vertical race, roughly 150 men, women, and teenagers race from the ground floor to the top of the Empire State Building in New York City. That's 1,576 steps, 86 floors, or 0.2 miles (0.3 km) in about 10 to 20 minutes!

In Skyscraper Run-Up, players multiply, divide, add, and subtract whole numbers to rise from floor to floor. Speed counts, of course, but so does accuracy. The five boards are multi-floor sections of a skyscraper. The answers on the top floor of each board follow a pattern. In other words, this game is conveniently self-checking. The boards present progressively harder skills as follows:

❋ **Skyscraper Run-Up 1: The 6th Floor!**
One- and two-digit multiplication, two-digit addition, one-digit subtraction and division; the final answer will always be 6.

❋ **Skyscraper Run-Up 2: 11th Heaven!**
Multiplying by 100, large number subtraction, long division; the final answer will always be 0.

❋ **Skyscraper Run-Up 3: Stuck on 12!**

Two-digit multiplication, one-and two-digit addition and subtraction, division by 10; the final
answer will always be the number on the 12th floor.

❋ **Skyscraper Run-Up 4: Zero Intolerance!**

One- and two-digit multiplication, multiplication by 10, two-digit addition, three-digit subtraction;
the final answer will always be the original number. (If the original number ended in 0,
remind players to follow the last step—multiply by 10—to get back to the original number.)

❋ **Skyscraper Run-Up 5: The Final Ride!**

Multiplication and division of two- and three-digit numbers; the final answer will always be the
original number. There are three answer check points along the way. Tell students that OG =
Original Number and FL = Floor.

After students have played a game, analyze the steps in each trick together. Use the number 1
as your original number to reveal how they work.

Skill Challenges

Here are two other ways to end the game.

❋ Set a time limit. The winner is the player who races the most numbers to the top before time
is up.

❋ Use all the numbers in the bag. The game ends when the last number is raced to the top.
The winner is the player who has raced the most numbers.

For both versions, players may need several copies of the board.

● Stage a classroom Skyscraper Run-Up contest. Students work in teams of two or three. Tape
together all five game boards to create a giant skyscraper. Players reenter their original number
each time they start a new section (between the 6th and 7th floors, the 11th and 12th floors, the
18th and 19th floors, and the 25th and 26th floors). The goal is to reach the roof first without
mistakes.

● Challenge students to add their own game boards to the Skyscraper Run-Up series. They can
modify the number tricks in the game, look for new number tricks in math puzzle books, or make
up their own tricks.

Skyscraper Run-Up

Players: 1 to 6 or more, plus a game monitor

SKILLS Mixed computation of whole numbers, mental math

MATERIALS
- Skyscraper Run-Up game board (one per player)
- bag of numbered sneakers (one per playing group)
- pencils and erasers (one per player)

Playing the Game

Accurately compute your way from the bottom to the top of a skyscraper as fast as you can.

1. Each player draws a numbered sneaker out of the bag. Don't look at the number until the game monitor says, "GO!"

2. When you hear the word "GO!" open your paper and look at the number. Write it in the first Original Number blank underneath the skyscraper.

3. Use the Original Number to make the calculation on the first floor. Write your answer in the first floor blank, directly above the Original Number.

Floor 1: Multiply by 4.	40
	Original Number: 10

4. Use the answer on the first floor to make the calculation on the second floor. Write the new answer in the second floor blank.

Floor 2: Add 25.	65
Floor 1: Multiply by 4.	40
	Original Number: 10

39

Skyscraper Run-Up

Players: 1 to 6 or more, plus a game monitor

5. Use the second floor answer to make the third floor calculation. Keep going until you reach the top floor on the board.

6. Quick! Draw a new numbered sneaker from the bag. Write this number in the second Original Number blank. Calculate your way to the top. Then draw a third number and, afterward, a fourth number.

7. To win, you must be the first player to reach the top for all four numbers without a single math mistake.

ONE-PLAYER RULES Race as many numbers in a row as you can without making a mistake. Then play again and try to beat your record.

MATH STRATEGY TIP Look for a pattern of numbers in the top floor answers.

NOTE: On The Final Ride! game board, these abbreviations are used:
OG means Original Number.
FL means Floor.
≠ means is not equal to.

Skyscraper Run-Up

Numbered Sneakers (*easier*)

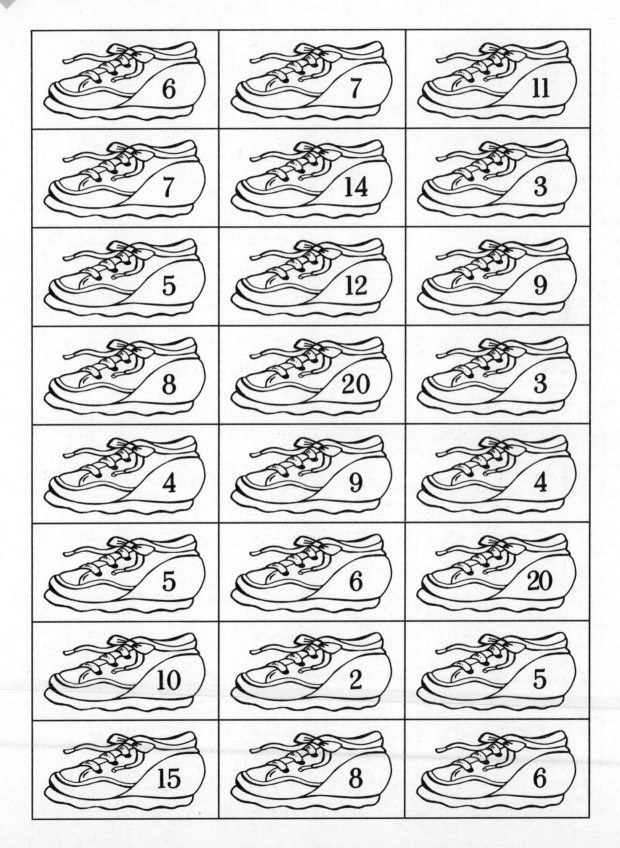

Skyscraper Run-Up

Numbered Sneakers (*harder*)

Skyscraper Run-Up!: 6th Floor!

Game Board

FLOOR 6	Subtract your original number.				
FLOOR 5	Divide by 8.				
FLOOR 4	Subtract 2.				
FLOOR 3	Multiply by 2.				
FLOOR 2	Add 25.				
FLOOR 1	Multiply by 4.				
		Original Number: _____	Original Number: _____	Original Number: _____	Original Number: _____

Skyscraper Run-Up 2: 11th Heaven!

Game Board

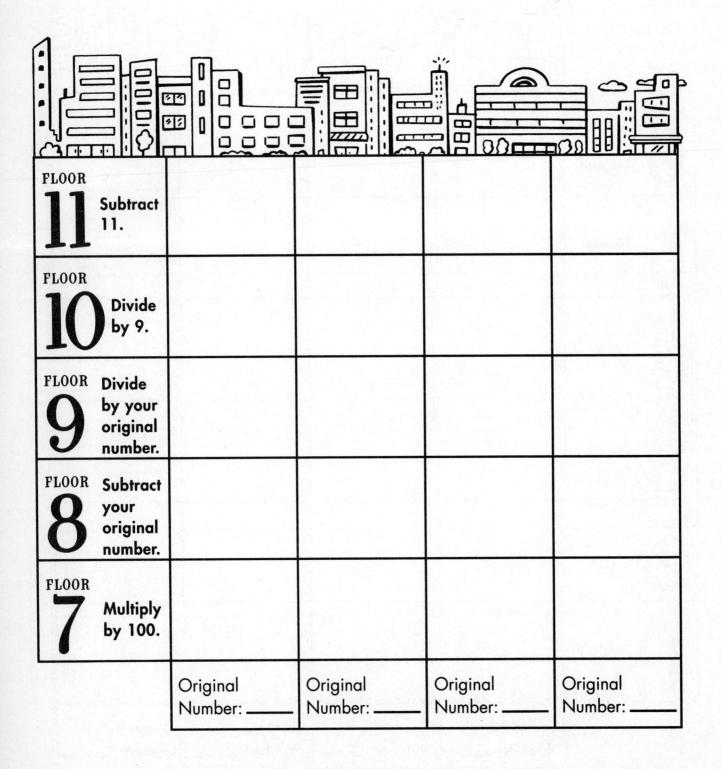

FLOOR **11** Subtract 11.				
FLOOR **10** Divide by 9.				
FLOOR **9** Divide by your original number.				
FLOOR **8** Subtract your original number.				
FLOOR **7** Multiply by 100.				
	Original Number: _____	Original Number: _____	Original Number: _____	Original Number: _____

Skyscraper Run-Up 3: Stuck On 12!

Game Board

FLOOR 18 Multiply by 5.				
FLOOR 17 Subtract 5.				
FLOOR 16 Divide by 10.				
FLOOR 15 Add 40.				
FLOOR 14 Multiply by 2.				
FLOOR 13 Add 5.				
FLOOR 12 Multiply by 5.				
	Original Number: _____	Original Number: _____	Original Number: _____	Original Number: _____

Skyscraper Run-Up 4: Zero Intolerence!

Game Board

FLOOR 25 Cross out 0's. If the OG ends in 0, x by 10.				
FLOOR 24 Subtract 320.				
FLOOR 23 Multiply by 10.				
FLOOR 22 Add 12.				
FLOOR 21 Multiply by 5.				
FLOOR 20 Add 4.				
FLOOR 19 Multiply by 2.				
	Original Number: _____	Original Number: _____	Original Number: _____	Original Number: _____

Skyscraper Run-Up 5: The Final Ride!

Game Board

ROOF Divide by 8.				
Floor 42 Divide by 9.				
Floor 41 Divide by 3.				
Floor 40 Multiply by 216.				
Floor 39 If FL 38 ≠ OG, back to FL 31.				
Floor 38 Divide by 13.				
Floor 37 Divide by 4.				
Floor 36 Divide by 3.				
Floor 35 Multiply by 156.				
Floor 34 If FL 38 ≠ OG, back to FL 26.				
Floor 33 Divide by 5.				
Floor 32 Divide by 12.				
Floor 31 Multiply by 60.				
Floor 30 If FL 29 ≠ OG, back to FL 26.				
Floor 29 Divide by 44.				
Floor 28 Multiply by 11.				
Floor 27 Divide by 9.				
Floor 26 Multiply by 36.				
	Original Number___	Original Number___	Original Number___	Original Number___

9 & 10 Gopher Golf & Mole Holes

Players: 1 or 2

Players travel from hole to hole by doing a chain of math problems. Their goal is to avoid making a single mistake and thus end up at 0 after visiting every hole.

SKILLS Mixed computation

PREPARATION Make one copy of the Gopher Golf or Mole Holes game board per game (pages 50-51) and one copy of the rules (page 49) per player. (Mole Holes has slightly tougher math problems, but game play is the same.) Provide each pair or solitaire player with counters (see page 5). Use half of one color or kind of counter and half of another for two-player games.

Basic Math Skills

Review with students how to check math problems by doing them backwards. For example, do an addition problem. Then subtract the first number from the sum. If this answer equals the second number, your sum is right.

Example:

$$\begin{array}{r} 1 \\ 59 \\ +\ 67 \\ \hline 126 \end{array}$$

Math check:

$$\begin{array}{r} 1\ 1 \\ 1\cancel{2}6 \\ -\ 67 \\ \hline 59 \end{array}$$

Skill Challenge

● Challenge students to create their own Gopher Golf or Mole Hole problems. Make sure there are no duplicate answers in the set.

Gopher Golf or Mole Holes

Players: 1 or 2

SKILLS Mixed computation

MATERIALS
- Gopher Golf or Mole Holes game board (one copy per game)
- counters (18 for Gopher Golf and 25 for Mole Holes)

Playing the Game

Chase a gopher or a mole from hole to hole by doing math problems. With no mistakes, you'll end up at 0—the only varmint-free place.

ONE PLAYER RULES 1. Begin at the hole marked "START." Do the math problem, and circle your answer. Cover the hole with a counter.

2. Look for the answer to your problem on another hole. (For instance, if your answer to 9 + 9 is 18, hunt for a problem with the number 18 in bold type. You will find the problem **18** + 28.) Do that problem. Circle your new answer, and cover that hole with a counter.

3. Continue following a chain of answers from one hole to the next.

4. Your goal is to cover every hole and end up at the flag with the 0 on it. If any hole is left uncovered, you have made a mistake. Start over.

TWO-PLAYER RULES Take turns doing the math problems. Work together to arrive at 0 without a single mistake.

MATH STRATEGY TIP Double-check your math on each problem.

Game Board

START

$\begin{array}{r} 9 \\ + 9 \\ \hline \end{array}$

$\begin{array}{r} 59 \\ + 9 \\ \hline \end{array}$

$\begin{array}{r} 100 \\ - 84 \\ \hline \end{array}$

$2\overline{)16}$

$2\overline{)46}$

$\begin{array}{r} 26 \\ + 94 \\ \hline \end{array}$

$\begin{array}{r} 8 \\ + 11 \\ \hline \end{array}$

0

$\begin{array}{r} 120 \\ - 61 \\ \hline \end{array}$

$\begin{array}{r} 11 \\ + 99 \\ \hline \end{array}$

$4\overline{)68}$

$\begin{array}{r} 19 \\ - 19 \\ \hline \end{array}$

$3\overline{)33}$

$\begin{array}{r} 69 \\ - 36 \\ \hline \end{array}$

$\begin{array}{r} 17 \\ \times 2 \\ \hline \end{array}$

$\begin{array}{r} 18 \\ + 28 \\ \hline \end{array}$

$\begin{array}{r} 23 \\ \times 3 \\ \hline \end{array}$

$\begin{array}{r} 34 \\ + 66 \\ \hline \end{array}$

$\begin{array}{r} 110 \\ - 84 \\ \hline \end{array}$

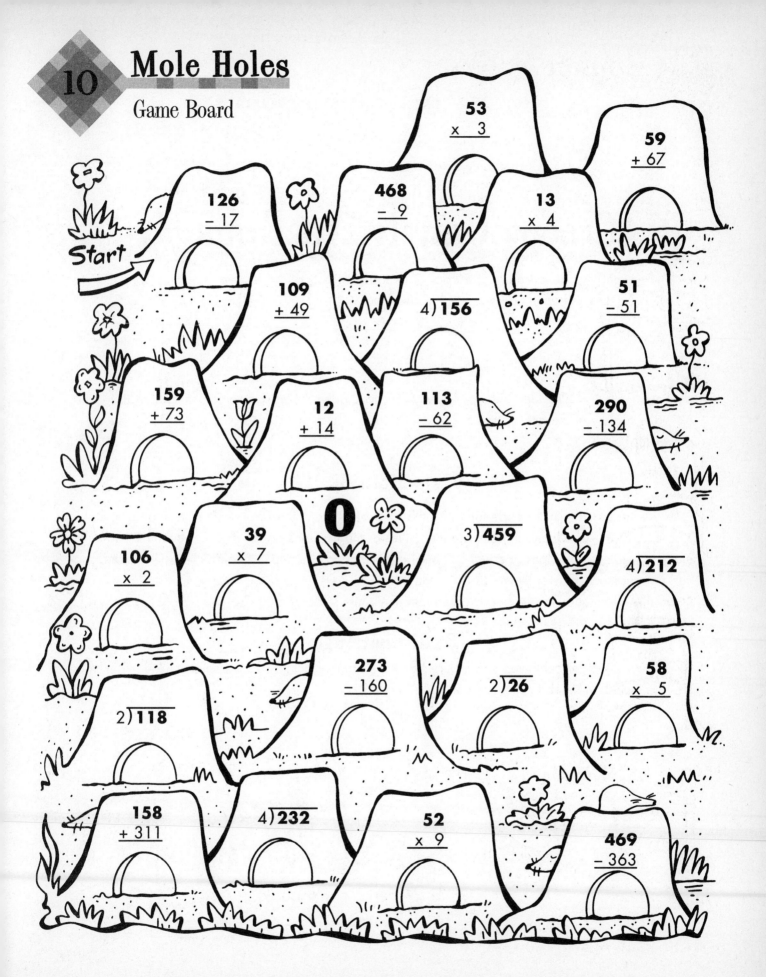

Mole Holes

10

Game Board

Start

126
− 17

468
− 9

53
x 3

13
x 4

59
+ 67

109
+ 49

4)156

51
− 51

159
+ 73

12
+ 14

113
− 62

290
− 134

106
x 2

39
x 7

0

3)459

4)212

2)118

273
− 160

2)26

58
x 5

158
+ 311

4)232

52
x 9

469
− 363

GAME 11 Creepy Crawly Fractions Players: 2 or more

Players advance along a track of 6-legged insects and 8-legged critters by spinning fractions and finding fraction equivalents.

SKILLS

Fraction equivalents

PREPARATION

Provide a Creepy Crawly Fractions game board (page 55), a spinner (page 54), and a copy of the rules (page 53) to each group of players. Have a place marker for each player (page 54).

Basic Math Skill

List all the possible sixths and eighths on the board (not including 0): $\frac{1}{6}, \frac{2}{6}, \frac{3}{6}, \frac{4}{6}, \frac{5}{6}, \frac{6}{6}$, and $\frac{1}{8}, \frac{2}{8}, \frac{3}{8}, \frac{4}{8}, \frac{5}{8}, \frac{6}{8}, \frac{7}{8}, \frac{8}{8}$. Ask students to compare the values of the fractions on the lists. For example, how many equivalents (fractions of equal amounts) can they find? ($\frac{3}{6}$ and $\frac{4}{8}$; $\frac{6}{6}$ and $\frac{8}{8}$) Which fractions can be renamed in lower terms? ($\frac{2}{6} = \frac{1}{3}$; $\frac{3}{6}$ and $\frac{4}{8} = \frac{1}{2}$; $\frac{4}{6} = \frac{2}{3}$; $\frac{6}{6}$ and $\frac{8}{8} = \frac{1}{1}$ or 1 ; $\frac{2}{8} = \frac{1}{4}$; $\frac{6}{8} = \frac{3}{4}$) Leave this information on the board as a reference while students play Creepy Crawly Fractions.

Skill Challenge

● Add a 12-legged centipede to the board and the simple fraction $\frac{1}{8}$ to the spinner. You might also want to include 4-legged critters and 2-legged critters.

Creepy Crawly Fractions

Players: 2 or more

SKILLS Fraction equivalents

MATERIALS
- Creepy Crawly Fractions game board
- Creepy Crawly spinner
- 2 or more place markers (one for each player)

Playing the Game

1. Put all place markers on "START."

2. To take a turn, spin the spinner to choose a fraction. Move your place marker ahead to the nearest equivalent (equal) fraction. Announce this fraction aloud as you land on it.

    ※ **Sample Turn 1:** You spin $\frac{1}{2}$. From "START," move ahead 1 space to the insect with 3 out of 6 ($\frac{3}{6}$) legs colored (1 move). Say "three-sixths" aloud.

    ※ **Sample Turn 2:** You spin $\frac{1}{3}$. Move ahead 3 spaces to the insect with 2 out of 6 ($\frac{2}{6}$) legs colored (3 moves). Say "one-third" aloud.

3. Players take turns spinning and moving. If a player moves to the wrong fraction, other players can challenge the move. The penalty for losing a challenge is to move back 1 space from the space where you started your turn.

4. The first player to reach the human at the "END" is the winner. Note that you must spin $\frac{1}{2}$ to win.

MATH STRATEGY TIP A 6-legged insect can have the equivalent fractions $\frac{2}{6}$ $(\frac{1}{3})$, $\frac{3}{6}$ $(\frac{1}{2})$, and $\frac{4}{6}$ $(\frac{2}{3})$. Spiders have 8 legs, and so can have the equivalent fractions $\frac{2}{8}$ $(\frac{1}{4})$, $\frac{4}{8}$ $(\frac{1}{2})$, and $\frac{6}{8}$ $(\frac{3}{4})$.

Creepy Crawly Fractions

Spinner

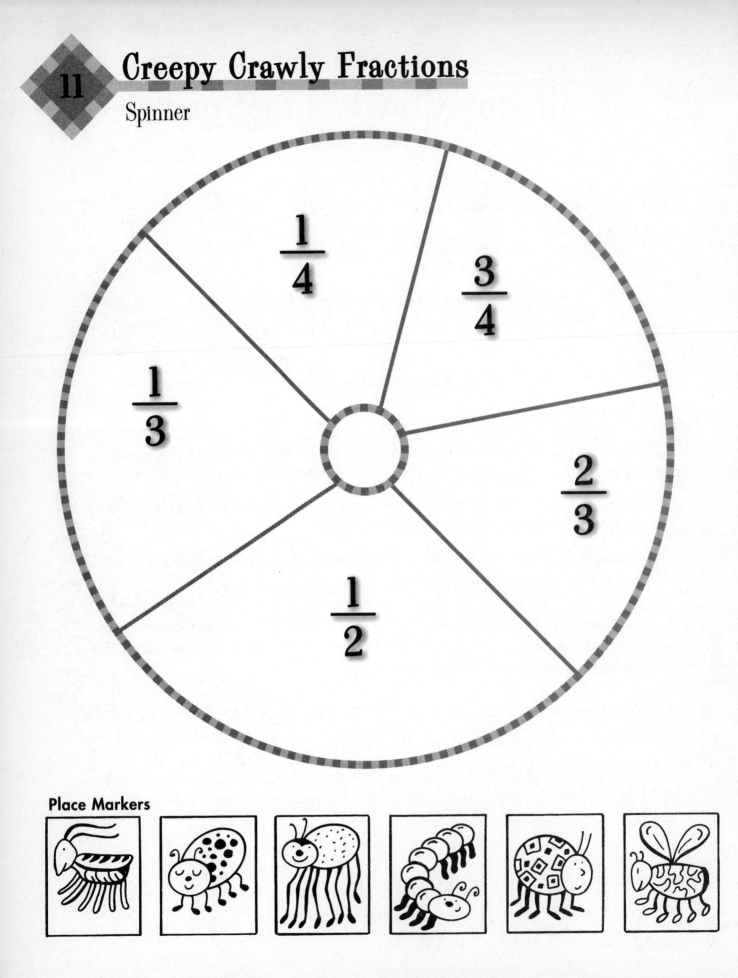

Place Markers

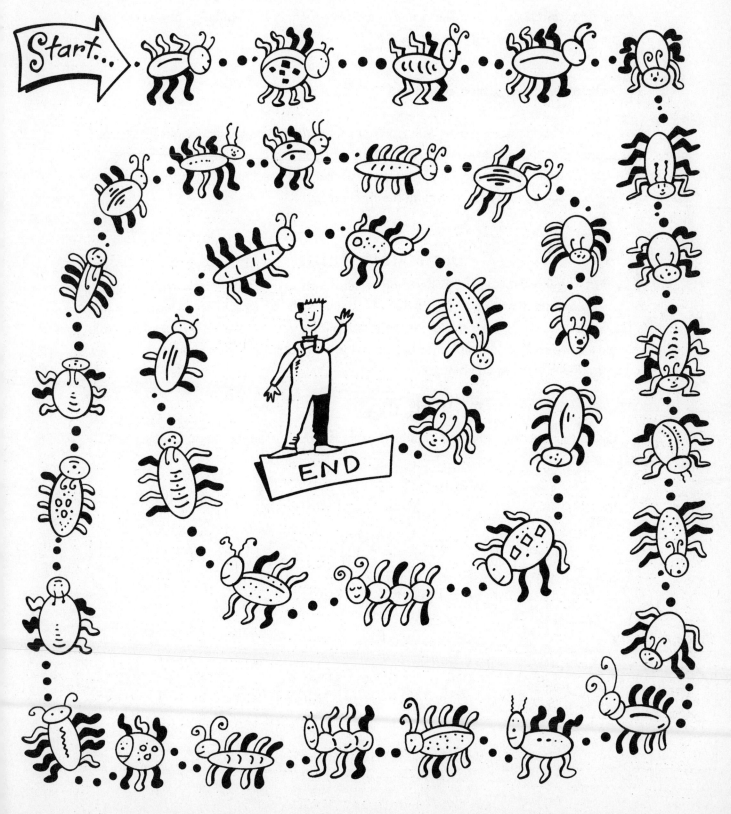

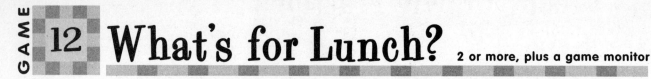

12 What's for Lunch?

2 or more, plus a game monitor

In this fraction equivalent version of Bingo, players must completely color three divided foods in a row. The game provides practice in identifying halves, thirds, fourths, sixths, and eighths.

SKILLS

Parts of a whole, fraction equivalents

PREPARATION

Provide each player with a What's for Lunch? Bingo card (page 59), a copy of the rules (page 57), and a marker or crayon. (Duplicate cards in the same game are okay, since players can choose which foods to color.) The game monitor will need the What's for Lunch? spinner (page 58), and scrap paper for recording the fractions spun.

Basic Math Skills

The tricky part of What's for Lunch? is deciding which foods to color in. For example, which foods can you color with a spin of $\frac{1}{1}$? (All of them.) Which foods are best to color for a spin of $\frac{1}{1}$? (Usually, a single food item, since 1 is the only spin that allows you to color it.) What other strategies do students discover? For example, it's best to color the middle space as soon as possible since it can form more winning combinations.

Skill Challenge

● Substitute more sixths and eighths for simple fractions on the Bingo Cards.

What's for Lunch?

Players: 2 or more, plus a game monitor

SKILLS Parts of a whole, fraction equivalents

MATERIALS

- What's for Lunch? Bingo cards (one page per player)
- What's for Lunch? spinner and scrap paper (for the game monitor)
- marker or crayon (one per player)

Playing the Game

Color three foods in a row to win!

1. The game monitor spins a fraction and says the results aloud. (He or she should write down each fraction in order to double-check the winning card.)

2. Color in the fraction or its equivalent on one of the foods on your card. For example, the monitor spins $\frac{1}{2}$. You could color half of one of these foods:

 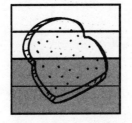 

3. A spin of $\frac{1}{1}$ means that you must color a whole food, even one divided into several parts.

4. For each fraction, you must color in the entire fraction amount. This means that you can't color any food on every spin. For example, the spinner lands on $\frac{1}{1}$, you can't color the pretzel. To complete the food, you need two spins of $\frac{1}{3}$.

5. When you have three squares in a row completely colored, say, "What's for Lunch?" The squares can be across, up-and-down, or diagonal.

6. The game monitor will check your answer. If your card is right, you win!

Spinner

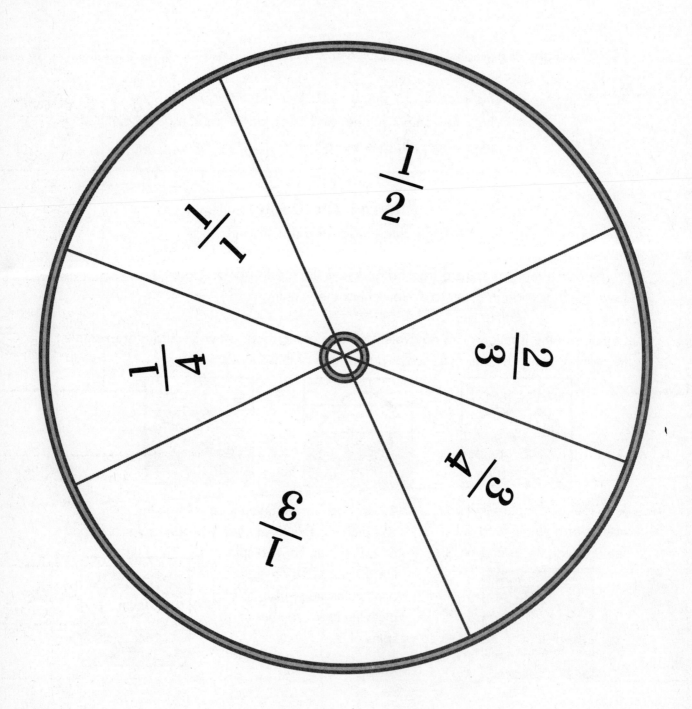

58

What's for Lunch?

Mouth-Watering Fraction Bingo

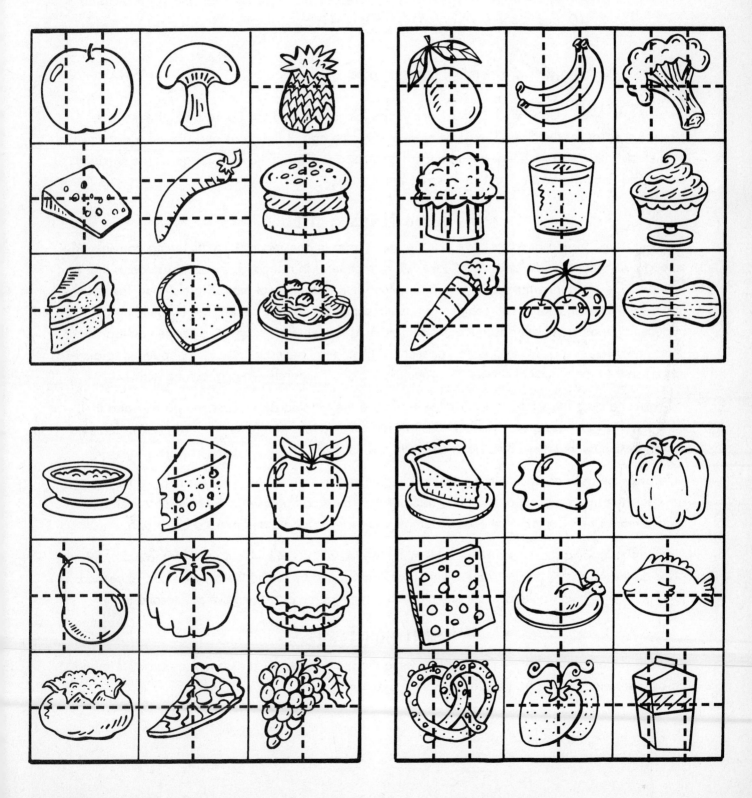

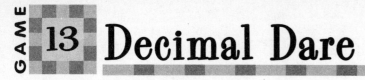

13 Decimal Dare

Players: 2 or more pairs of players, plus a game monitor

Pairs of players perform simple dares, such as tapping their fingers as fast as they can. They count, record, and graph the repetitions in 10 seconds and, after dividing by 10, in 1 second.

SKILLS
Dividing by 10, averaging, graphing data

PREPARATION
Copy the Decimal Dare Cards (page 63) onto tag board and cut them out; one set of cards for the class. The game monitor takes charge of the cards and also of a stopwatch or a clock with a second hand. Each pair will also need a copy of the rules (page 61), a Decimal Dare Data Sheet (page 62), and some scrap paper.

Basic Math Skills

Ask students: *How many times can you tap your finger in one second?* Try it! Timing one second is tough. Just saying "Go" and "Stop" takes up a fraction of that second. Explain to students that a better way to measure what happens in one second is to use decimal math. Here's how: Tap your finger for 10 seconds and then compute an average number of taps per second by dividing by 10. In decimal terms, move the decimal point one place to the left. For example, suppose you tap 55 times in 10 seconds. That's 5.5 times per second! (If students have not yet been introduced to decimals, use the whole number scores—the repetitions per 10 seconds—throughout the activity.)

Divide the class into pairs, and have them practice the tapping dare—first one partner and then the other. How close are everyone's scores? Based on the class's tapping data, what other feats do students estimate that they could do in less than one second?

Arrange the pairs of players in a circle and begin the game. After everyone has finished the dares, have students make a bar graph of their results. Which feats can people do the fastest? Which ones require more time? Compute the class's average score for each dare and make a bar graph.

Example: Tapping scores per 10 seconds might be 34, 37, 40, 41, 42, 45, 50, 50, 52, 57, 57, 60. Add the 12 scores (total = 565). Divide by 12 and round off to find the average per 10 seconds (565 ÷ 12 = 47). Move the decimal one place to the left for the average score per second (4.7).

Skill Challenge

● Have students add their own Decimal Dares to the set of cards, such as bouncing a ball, flipping cards in a deck, picking up pennies, jumping rope, and so on.

Decimal Dare

**Players: 2 or more pairs of
players, plus a game monitor**

SKILLS Dividing by 10, averaging, graphing data

MATERIALS
- Decimal Dare Data Sheet
- Decimal Dare Cards (for the game monitor)
- scrap paper
- pen or pencil
- stopwatch or clock with second hand
- calculator (optional)

Playing the Game

Work with your partner to repeat a dare as many times as you can in 10 seconds. Divide your scores by 10 to find your average repetitions per second.

1. The game monitor will pass out a Decimal Dare Card to each pair of players.

2. Decide which partner will do the first dare. Then wait for the game monitor to say "GO!". One partner has 10 seconds to repeat the dare as many times as possible. The other partner counts the repetitions.

3. Record the total on the Data Sheet. Divide the total by 10. Then record this number under Repetitions Per Second.

4. Pass your dare to the next pair of students. Another pair of students will hand you a new dare. Partners switch doing dares and counting repetitions.

5. After all the dares have been passed around, add your final score. Here are two ways to do it:
   ※ Add the whole numbers in the Total Repetitions column. Divide the total by 10.
   ※ Add the decimal figures in the Repetitions per Second column. (Use a calculator to check your work.)

MATH STRATEGY TIP To divide by 10, just move the decimal point one place to the left; for example, $55 \div 10 = 5.5$.

Decimal Dare

Data Sheet

Dare	Total Repetitions	Repetitions per Second (÷ 10)
1		
2		
3		
4		
5		
6		
7		
8		
9		
10		
11		
12		

Total Score: _____

Decimal Dare

Cards

1 **Decimal Dare!** Lay either hand flat on the table. Tap your pinky (little finger) up and down.	**2** **Decimal Dare!** Write the word DARE over and over. Each word must be legible (readable).	**3** **Decimal Dare!** Clasp and unclasp your hands. All fingers must inter-lock and then straighten out.
4 **Decimal Dare!** Say "Fee, fi, fo, fum" over and over. Saying all four words counts as one repetition.	**5** **Decimal Dare!** Write the word ME over and over. Each word must be legible (readable).	**6** **Decimal Dare!** Say "I think, therefore I am" over and over. Each sentence counts as one repetition.
7 **Decimal Dare!** Fold a sheet of notebook paper in half two times. Then unfold it.	**8** **Decimal Dare!** Draw a five-pointed star over and over. Each star counts as one repetition.	**9** **Decimal Dare!** Do jumping jacks. One repetition equals two steps—step out and step in.
10 **Decimal Dare!** Tap either foot on the floor over and over.	**11** **Decimal Dare!** Write any three letters over and over. Each set of three counts as one repetition.	**12** **Decimal Dare!** Say "Do re me fa so la ti" over and over. Each set of seven syllables is one repetition.
13 **Decimal Dare!** Make up your own dare! _____ _____	**14** **Decimal Dare!** Make up your own dare! _____ _____	**15** **Decimal Dare!** Make up your own dare! _____ _____

14 Decimal Dives

Players: 2 to 4

Players spin the spinner to claim the highest-scoring decimals in four Olympic diving events. After all scores have been claimed, the high scorer in each event wins the event. Up to four players can win a gold medal!

SKILLS
Decimal inequalities, decimal addition

PREPARATION
Provide each playing group with a Decimal Dives game board (pages 68–69), a spinner (page 67), a rule sheet (pages 65–66), scrap paper, and 36 counters (for two players, use 18 of one color or kind and 18 of another; for three players, use three colors or kinds; for four players, use four colors or kinds). Have students tape two pages of the game board together.

Basic Math Skills

To warm up for the event, work as a class to order the scores from the lowest to the highest in one of the diving events. Challenge students to order a second event on their own. (If students are unfamiliar with decimals, change the diving scores to whole numbers by eliminating the decimal points.)

For practice in adding columns of decimals, instruct students to choose the International Scoring rules (See page 66). Review how to line up decimal points before adding:

$$\begin{array}{r} {}^{1}9.7 \\ +\ 8.6 \\ \hline 18.3 \end{array}$$

Students can check their work with calculators.

Skill Challenge

● Change the sport to gymnastics and introduce scores in the hundredths place (7.69, for example). The events could include floor exercise, vault, uneven bars (girls) or parallel bars (boys), and balance beam (girls) or rings (boys).

Decimal Dives

Players: 2 to 4

SKILLS Decimal inequalities, decimal addition

MATERIALS
- Decimal Dives game board (Tape two pages together.)
- Decimal Dives spinner
- scrap paper (for tallying scores)
- 36 counters (an even number per diver; each diver has a different kind of counter)
- calculator (optional; for checking the International Scoring)

Playing the Game

Who can claim the highest-scoring dives in each event?

1. To take a turn, spin the spinner. Find the table that matches the event that you spin. Place one of your counters on any unmarked dive . If you spin "Choose any event", place your counter on any open dive on the game board.

2. If you spin "Scratch a dive", remove any one of your counters from the board. (If you don't have any dives yet, you get to spin again.)

3. If you spin an event that is full (no open diving scores), spin again.

4. The game ends when the first player runs out of counters.

5. Score each event separately.

Easy Scoring: You need at least three dives to win an event. Throw out your highest and lowest dives. The player with the highest remaining score wins the event.

Example: You score 9.3, 8.3, 7.4, and 6.7 in the 3-Meter Springboard. Throw out 9.3 and 6.7 Your score for that event is 8.3—the next highest score still left.

Decimal Dives

Players: 2

International Scoring: You need at least two dives to win an event. For each event, calculate your average score. Here's how: Add the scores. Then divide by the number of dives. The player with the highest average score in each event wins the event. Use calculator to check work.

Example: You score 9.7, 9.5, and 8.6 in the 10-Meter Platform.

Line up the decimals and add the scores

$$
\begin{array}{r}
9.7 \\
9.5 \\
+\ 8.6 \\
\hline
27.8 \\
\end{array}
$$

Divide by 3 (the number of dives).

$$
\begin{array}{r}
9.26 \\
3\overline{)27.80} \\
-27 \\
\hline
8 \\
6 \\
\hline
20 \\
18 \\
\hline
2 \\
\end{array}
$$

Your score for the 10-meter platform is 9.27 (rounded to the nearest hundredth).

MATH STRATEGY TIP

To check which decimal is the highest, first compare the number farthest to the left (usually the ones place). If they're the same, then compare the number second to the left (usually the tenths place).

Example:

6.82

6.97

The numbers in the ones place are the same. In the tenths place, 0.9 is higher than the 0.8. So 6.97 is the higher number.

14

Decimal Dives

Spinner

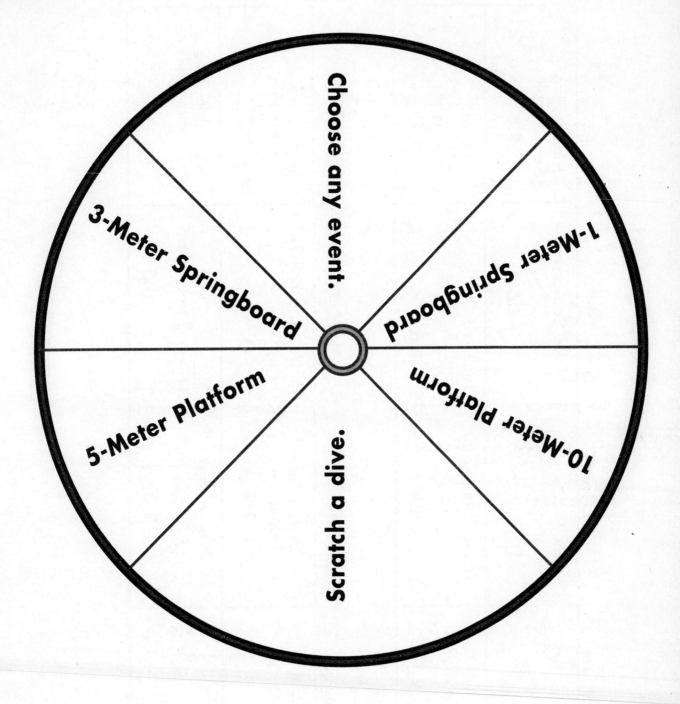

Decimal Dives

Game Board

10-Meter Platform

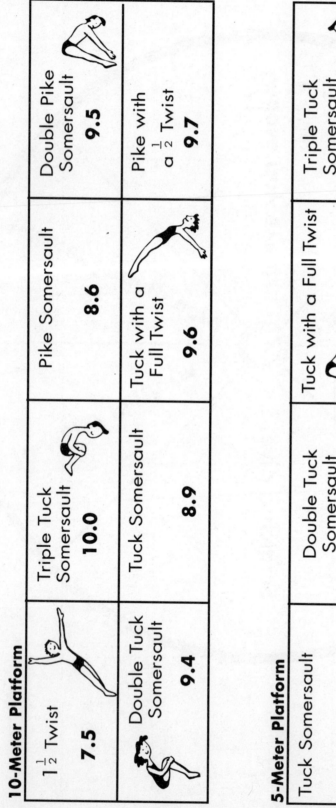

		Double Pike Somersault **9.5**
Triple Tuck Somersault **10.0**	Pike Somersault **8.6**	Pike with a ½ Twist **9.7**
Double Tuck Somersault **9.4**	Tuck Somersault **8.9**	Tuck with a Full Twist **9.6**
1½ Twist **7.5**		

5-Meter Platform

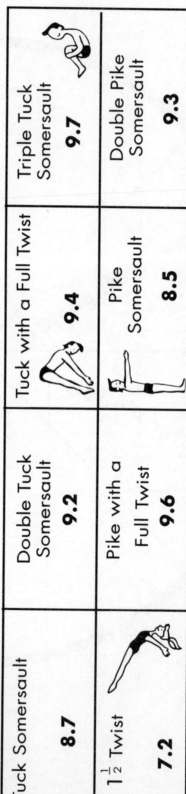

	Triple Tuck Somersault **9.7**
Tuck with a Full Twist **9.4**	Double Pike Somersault **9.3**
Double Tuck Somersault **9.2**	Pike Somersault **8.5**
Tuck Somersault **8.7**	
1½ Twist **7.2**	Pike with a Full Twist **9.6**

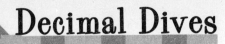

14 Decimal Dives

Game Board

3-Meter Springboard

Full Twist 6.9 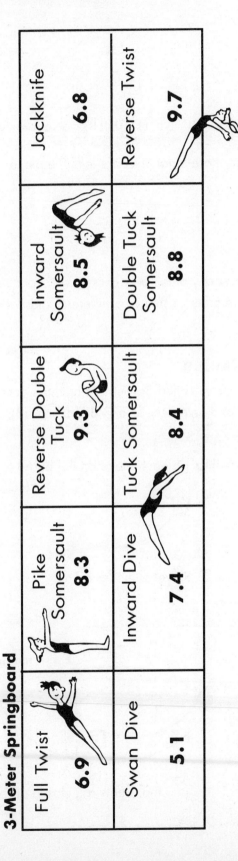	Pike Somersault 8.3	Reverse Double Tuck 9.3	Jackknife 6.8
Swan Dive 5.1	Inward Dive 7.4	Tuck Somersault 8.4	Reverse Twist 9.7

1-Meter Springboard

Tuck Somersault 8.2 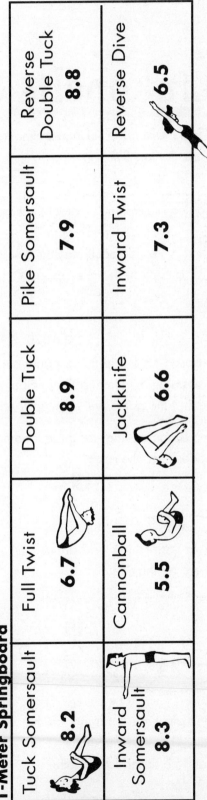	Full Twist 6.7	Double Tuck 8.9	Reverse Double Tuck 8.8
Inward Somersault 8.3	Cannonball 5.5	Jackknife 6.6	Reverse Dive 6.5 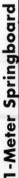

G A M E
15 # Linkopolis A Geometric Metropolis   **Players: 2 or 3**

Players take turns linking landmarks until no more legal links are left. The player to make the last link wins.

SKILLS
Topology, graphing, logical thinking

PREPARATION
Provide each playing group with one copy of the Linkopolis game board per game (page 73), a copy of the rules (page 72), and a marker or pen of a different color for each player.

Basic Skill Review

Linkopolis is based on a traditional paper-and-pencil game called Sprouts. At first, the possible plays seem endless, but by limiting the number of exits and entrances to an odd number (3), the rules guarantee that the game will eventually end.

Here's a sample game using just three landmarks. Play through each move on the board to make sure students understand the rules.

1. Player 1 makes the first link and draws a dot anywhere on the line.

2. Player 2 makes a link.

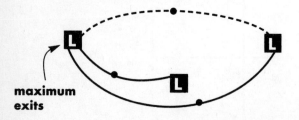

3. Player 1's link gives the landmark on the left three exits. That's the maximum. The landmark can't be linked to any other landmarks or dots.

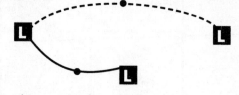

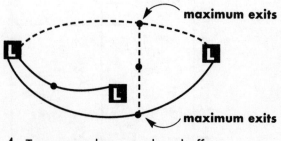

4. Two more dots are closed off.

15 Linkopolis A Geometric Metropolis   Players: 2 or 3

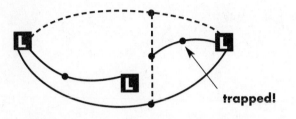

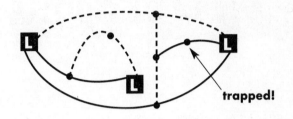

5. Player 1's new dot is trapped inside. It can't link with any other landmark without illegally crossing a line.

6. Player 2's moves are limited to the only two landmarks with available links.

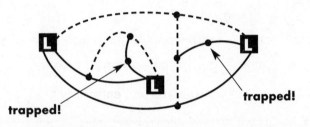

7. Player 1 wins by trapping another dot inside the lines.

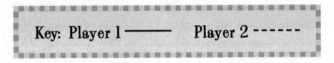

Key: Player 1 ———— Player 2 ------

Skill Challenge

● Combine two Linkopolis boards into a single game.

Linkopolis

Players: 2 or 3

SKILLS Topology, graphing, logical thinking

MATERIALS
- Linkopolis game board (one copy per game)
- 2 or 3 pens or markers of different colors (one per player)

Playing the Game

Keep linking the landmarks with roads until no legal link is left.

1. To take a turn, draw a link between any two landmarks. Then draw a new landmark (a dot) anywhere along this new road. Follow these rules:

- The road can't cross another road.
- The road can't pass through a landmark. (All links start or stop at a landmark.)
- No landmark can have more than 3 roads going in or out of it.

Examples of illegal moves:

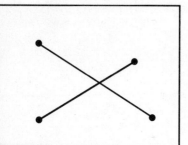 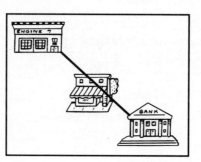 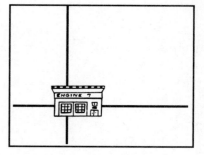

2. Dots are new landmarks, so you can link a dot to a pictured landmark or link a dot to a dot. Like the original landmarks, the new landmarks (or dots) can have only 3 exits.

3. The last player to make a legal link wins.

MATH STRATEGY TIP Linked lines don't have to be straight. Experiment with curves. Also, you can link any two landmarks, no matter how far apart. Just don't cross over another link or pass through a third landmark.

15

Linkopolis

Game Board

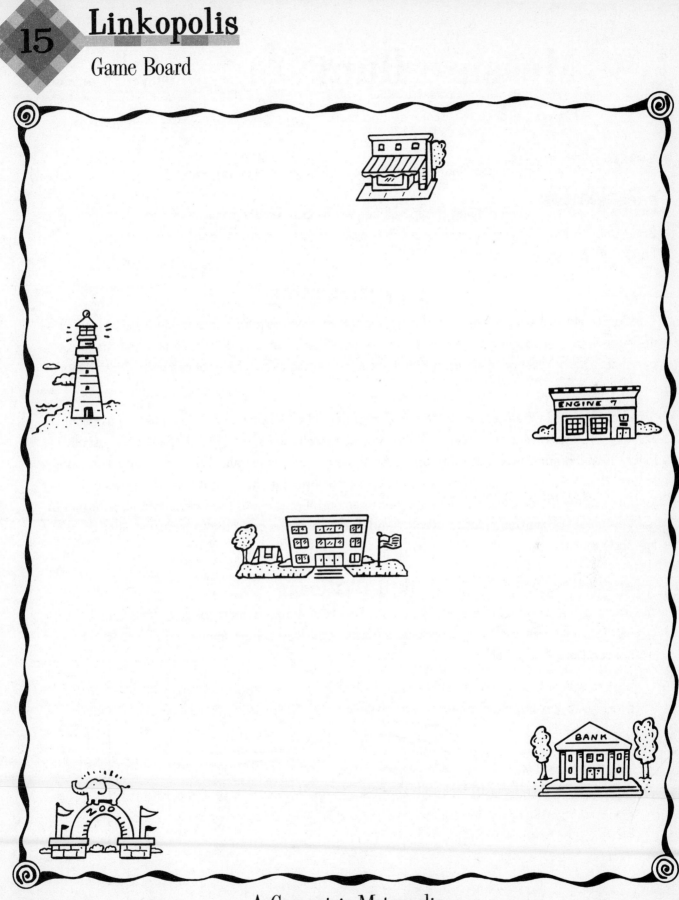

A Geometric Metropolis

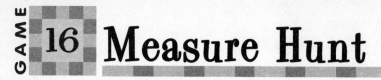

GAME

16 Measure Hunt

Players: 2 or more

Players advance by estimating and measuring length in units called Bones.

SKILLS Measuring and estimating length, metric measurements, rounding

PREPARATION Each playing group will need a Measure Hunt game board (page 77), a set of Bone Units (page 76), a counter, two or more place markers, a watch or clock with a second hand, and a copy of the rules (page 75).

Basic Math Skills

Measure Hunt alternates between asking students to estimate length and to measure objects to the nearest unit. As a warm-up exercise, have each student cut a string the same length as his or her shoe. Then challenge students to find three things in the classroom that are very close to that length.

Measurements in the Measure Hunt game must be within 1 Bone Unit (3 centimeters) to count. For "Body Checks," the arm span and height are generally the same. The shoe length is usually longer than the hand span (although about the same as the foot length). The middle finger is usually longer than the nose. The hand span is usually longer than the chin to hairline. The forearm is longer than the hand span. If a student's measurements turn out to be too close to call, give him or her the benefit of the doubt. Demonstrate hand and arm spans and how to measure other parts of the body as necessary.

Skill Challenge

● Create a similar game to measure capacity. Locate uniform counters (beads, dried beans, or rice, for example) and various containers (small cups, tray compartments, egg cartons, empty film canisters, and so on) to fill with the counters.

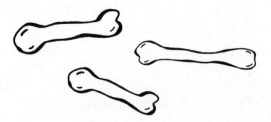

Measure Hunt

Players: 2 or more

SKILLS Measuring and estimating length, metric measurements, rounding

MATERIALS
- Measure Hunt game board
- Bone Unit set (or ruler)
- 2 or more place markers (one for each player)
- 1 counter
- watch or clock with a second hand
- box of objects to measure
- scrap paper and pencil (to keep score)

Playing the Game

Measure your way from toe to head on the giant skeleton!

1. Put your place marker on "START."

2. For each turn, the player on your left hides a counter in either hand. Choose the player's right or left hand. If the hand contains the counter, move ahead 2 spaces. If it does not contain the counter, move 1 space.

3. Follow the directions on the space where you land.

Measure Hunt: You have 10 seconds. (Have another player time you.) Find an object whose length or width is within one Bone Unit of the number on the space. Score 5 points if you succeed.

Estimation Station: Pick any object. Estimate its length in Bone Units. Then measure it to the nearest Bone Unit. Score 5 points if your estimate is correct within 1 Bone Unit. Subtract 1 point for every Bone Unit that your estimate is off. **Example:** You estimate 6 Bone Units. The object is just under 5 Bone Units. You score 4 points (5 – 1 = 4).

Body Check: Are the two body lengths equal? If not, guess which body length is longer. Measure the lengths in Bone Units. If you're right, score 3 points.

4. Once an object has been measured, it is out of play.

5. The game ends after all players have reached the "END." The player with the most points wins.

 Measure Hunt

Measure Hunt Bone Units

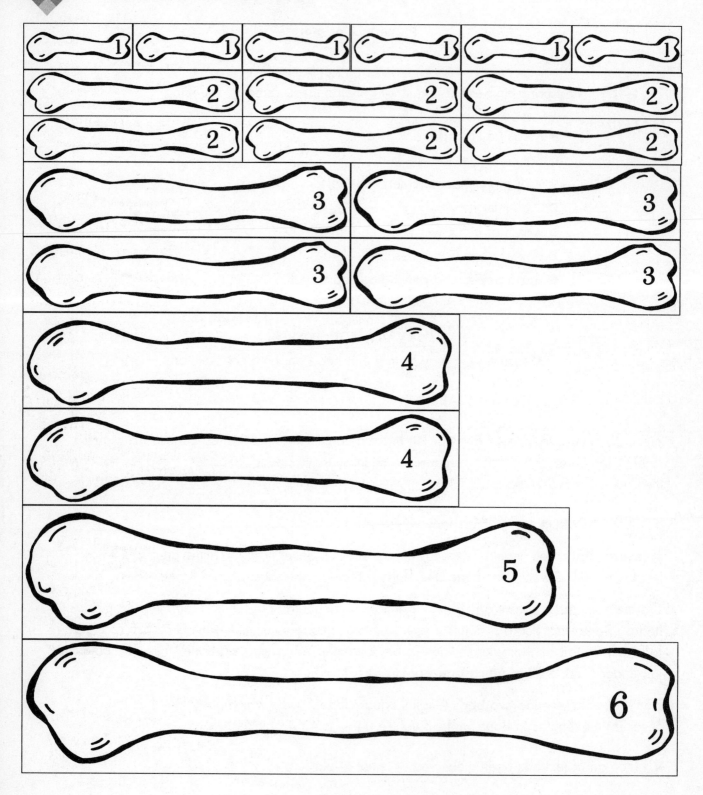

16

Measure Hunt

Game Board

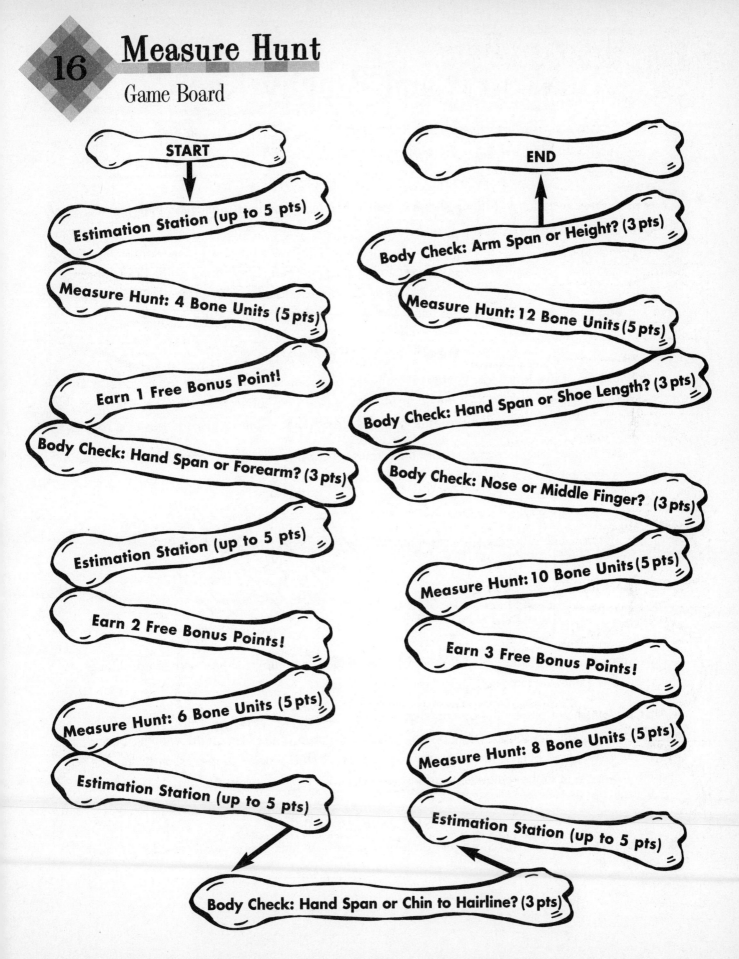

START

Estimation Station (up to 5 pts)

Measure Hunt: 4 Bone Units (5 pts)

Earn 1 Free Bonus Point!

Body Check: Hand Span or Forearm? (3 pts)

Estimation Station (up to 5 pts)

Earn 2 Free Bonus Points!

Measure Hunt: 6 Bone Units (5 pts)

Estimation Station (up to 5 pts)

Body Check: Hand Span or Chin to Hairline? (3 pts)

END

Body Check: Arm Span or Height? (3 pts)

Measure Hunt: 12 Bone Units (5 pts)

Body Check: Hand Span or Shoe Length? (3 pts)

Body Check: Nose or Middle Finger? (3 pts)

Measure Hunt: 10 Bone Units (5 pts)

Earn 3 Free Bonus Points!

Measure Hunt: 8 Bone Units (5 pts)

Estimation Station (up to 5 pts)

Snake Pit and Peachy Keen

Players: 1 or 2

Players take turns filling their Snake Pits or Peach Orchards with tiles of various shapes. The winner is the player who fills the most area.

SKILLS

Area, translation (sliding shapes), rotation (spinning shapes), reflection (flipping shapes), visual perception

PREPARATION

Snake Pit is an easier version of Peachy Keen. Choose the game board (page 81 or 83, rules (page 79), and tiles (pages 80 or 82) appropriate for your students. Copy the tiles onto tag board, cut out along the solid lines, and laminate them for longer use.

Basic Skill Review

Distribute four or five identical squares to each pair of students. Challenge the teams to form as many four-unit or five-unit shapes as they can. All shapes must be connected along the sides, not by the corners of the squares. The easiest shape is a straight line—four or five squares in a row.

The Snake Pit tiles include examples of all the four-unit shapes possible. Peachy Keen tiles include most of the five-unit shapes. Did students come up with others? Here are two:

Demonstrate how to rotate (spin), translate (slide), and reflect (flip) a shape. When translating shapes in the game, students can "hop over" other shapes.

After students have played the games, discuss their strategies for winning. What is the area of each board? (Count the squares to find out.) What is the area of the tiles on the winning board? (Count the tiles to find out.) Which tiles are easiest to use? (The simpler shapes, such as the line and the L-shapes, fit in the rectangular grid better.)

Skill Challenge

● Change the snake pit or orchard into an irregular area. Which shapes work best for the new areas?

Snake Pit or Peachy Keen

Players: 1 or 2

SKILLS Area, translation (sliding shapes), rotation (spinning shapes), reflection (flipping shapes), visual perception

MATERIALS
- Snake Pit or Peachy Keen game board
- Snake or peach tree tiles

Playing the Game
Who can cover the most area?

1. Each player chooses a pit or an orchard to fill. Lay out all the tiles so that both players can see and reach them.

2. To take a turn, make one of these moves:
   - Choose any tile in the pile and place it in your area. You can rotate (spin) or reflect (flip) it before you put it down.
   - Rotate, translate, or reflect a tile that's already in your area. After you change it, you can place it anywhere that it fits.
   - Remove a tile from your area and return it to the pile.

3. Each tile must fit inside a square. No two tiles can overlap.

4. The game ends when one player has filled his or her entire area. In Peachy Keen, the last move is to place your barn tile in the last remaining area.

ONE-PLAYER RULES How long does it take to cover every space in an area? Time yourself. Then try to beat your best time.

MATH STRATEGY TIP Experiment with starting in the middle versus starting at the edges. Plan several moves ahead. Rotate (spin), translate (slide), or reflect (flip) shapes to make room for new shapes. Pay attention to your opponent's area. You may be able to block his or her play by hanging on to certain tiles.

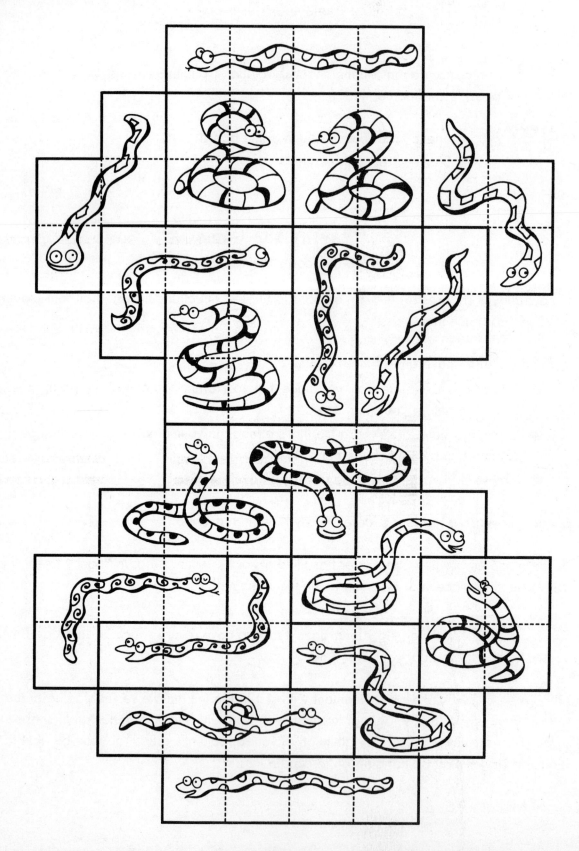

80

Snake Pit

17

Game Board

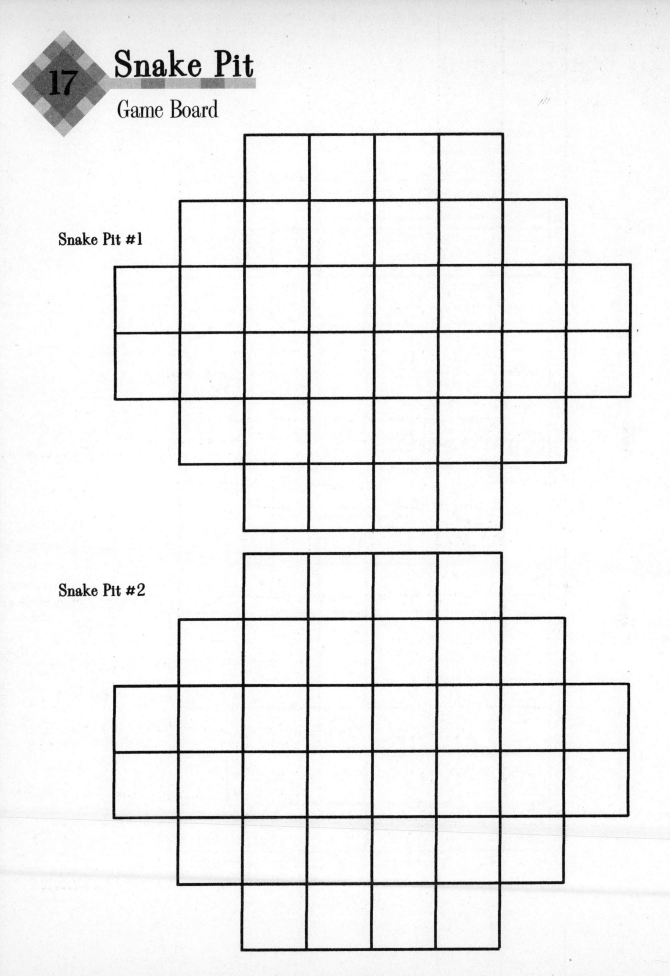

Snake Pit #1

Snake Pit #2

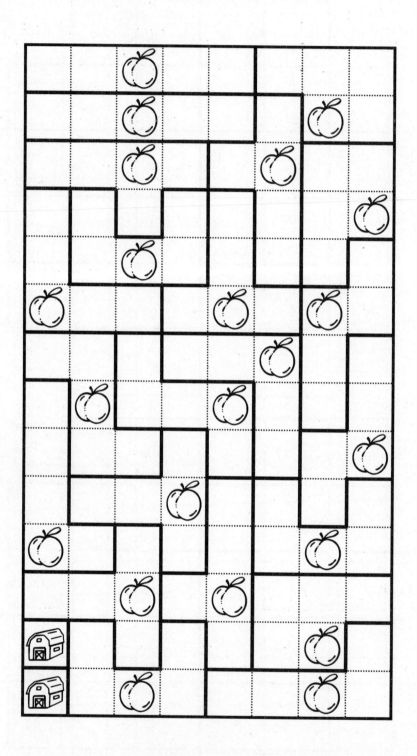

Peachy Keen

Game Board

Sweet Georgia Grounds

Peach Blossom Paradise

G A M E

19 Easy Street

Players: 2 to 6

Players cruise through life by choosing and spinning the luckiest path (the one they are most likely to spin).

SKILLS Calculating probability, logical operators (the words *and* and *or*)

PREPARATION Provide each playing group with an Easy Street game board (page 87), an Easy Street spinner (page 86), and a copy of the rules (page 85). Cut out a place marker below for each player.

Basic Math Skills

After students play Easy Street, discuss their discoveries about probability. Which events are most likely to happen? (finding $10 or a lost kitten) What are the chances of spinning each event? (1 out of 2) What are the chances of spinning other events? ("Meet a Movie Star" or "Find $100": 1 out of 3, "Win the Lottery" or "Play Pro Sports": 1 out of 6) How many times more likely is a player to "Find $10" than "Win the Lottery"? (3 times—3 out of 6 chances versus 1 out of 6 chances)

The words *and* and *or* have special meaning in the world of logic. Students may have used these terms while doing a computer search, for example. How does using the word *and* or *or* affect the chances of something happening? Which has a greater chance of happening: Meeting a Movie Star and Winning the Lottery versus Meeting a Movie Star or Winning the Lottery? (Just as in a computer search, the word *or* includes more possibilities while the word *and* reduces possibilities.)

Skill Challenge

● Challenge students to create their own Easy Street game.

Easy Street Place Markers

Easy Street

Players: 2 to 6

SKILLS Calculating probability, logical operators (the words *and* and *or*)

MATERIALS
- Easy Street game board
- Easy Street spinner
- 2 to 6 place markers (one for each player)

Playing the Game

Cruise through life by choosing and spinning the luckiest path.

1. Place all place markers on "START HERE."

2. To take a turn, choose one of the two events in 1 ("Find $10" or "Find a Kitten"). Place your marker on that space. Then spin the spinner.

Does the spin match the event that you chose?

   ※ If not, your turn is over.

   ※ If so, move ahead to either of the events in 2 and end your turn.

3. Before spinning for your next turn, you can stay where you are or move to the other event on the same level.

4. Take turns until the winning player reaches "Easy Street" first.

MATH STRATEGY TIP Some events (finding $10) are easier to achieve than others (winning the lottery). Don't get greedy. Take the easy path if you want the best chance to get ahead.

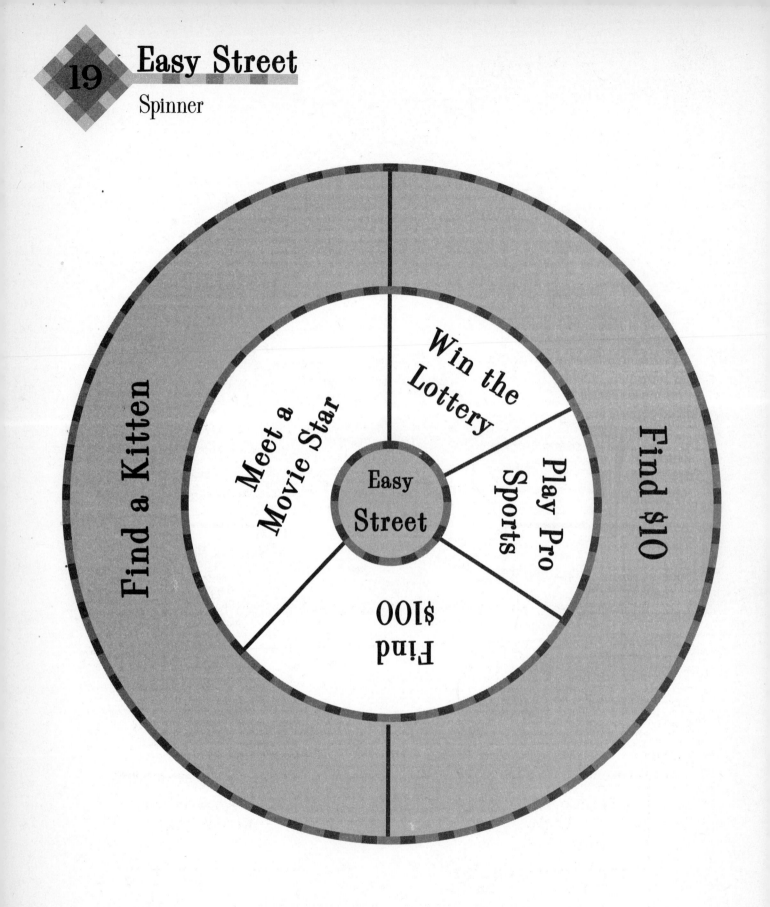

Find a Kitten

Meet a Movie Star

Win the Lottery

Play Pro Sports

Find $10

Easy Street

Find $100

Easy Street

Game Board

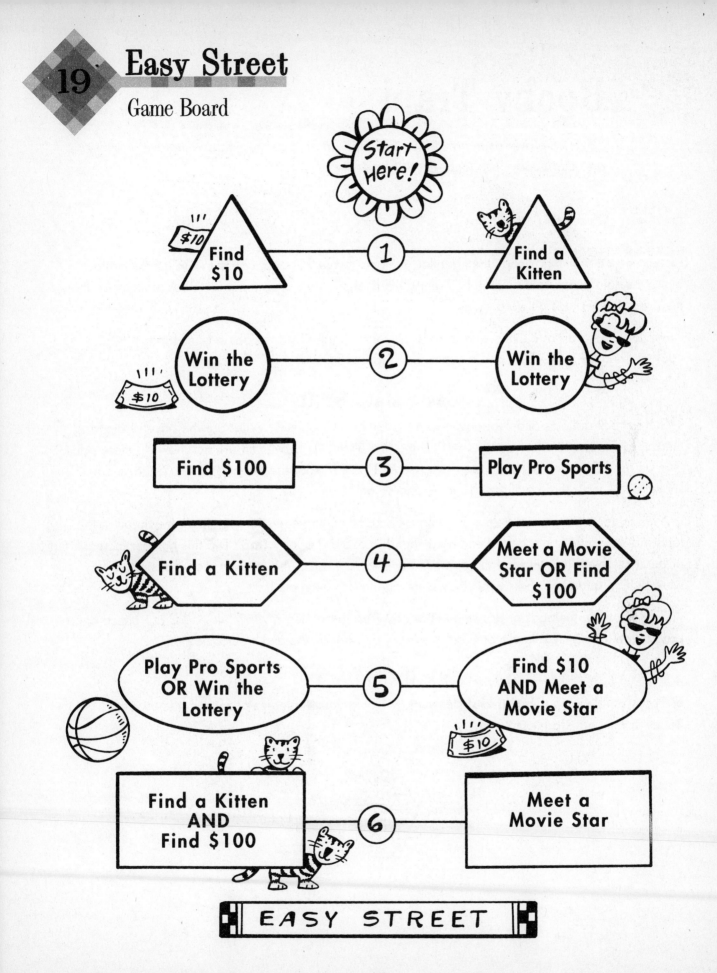

Start Here!

1   Find $10 — Find a Kitten

2   Win the Lottery — Win the Lottery

3   Find $100 — Play Pro Sports

4   Find a Kitten — Meet a Movie Star OR Find $100

5   Play Pro Sports OR Win the Lottery — Find $10 AND Meet a Movie Star

6   Find a Kitten AND Find $100 — Meet a Movie Star

EASY STREET

20 Booby Trap!

Players flip over as many hidden Egyptian artifacts as they dare while avoiding the dreaded Booby Trap (cobra).

SKILLS
Calculating probability

PREPARATION
Photocopy the Egyptian artifacts (page 90) onto oak tag. Cut out the artifacts along the solid lines. Fold them in half along the dashed lines. Glue the plain sides together so that the printed sides face outward.

Provide each pair of players with a set of artifacts, the Booby Trap game board (page 92), a copy of the rules (page 89), and a Score Sheet (page 91).

Basic Math Skills

There are 9 artifacts and 1 Booby Trap for a total of 10 objects. What are the odds of drawing the Booby Trap on the first try? (1 in 10) If the first player turns over an artifact, how do these odds change for the second player? (They increase to 1 in 9.) What are the odds if two artifacts are showing? (1 in 8) three artifacts? (1 in 7, and so on).

After students have played several rounds, discuss their strategies for winning. How many artifacts did they usually flip before ending a round to avoid a Booby Trap? Did this number increase or decrease over the course of the game? Why? (Students may have taken more risks when they were behind and fewer risks when they were ahead, for example.)

Does knowing the odds of drawing the Booby Trap guarantee a win? (No, odds are based on probability—the probable outcome of an event—and not on the exact outcome.)

Skill Challenge

● Pose the following question to students: How would your strategies change if there were 2 Booby Traps and 8 artifacts? Try it!

Booby Trap!

Players: 2

SKILLS Calculating probability

MATERIALS
- Booby Trap! Score Sheet
- 10 Egyptian artifacts
- Booby Trap! game board

Playing the Game

How many hidden Egyptian objects do you dare to flip over? Watch out! The dreaded Booby Trap is lurking among them!

1. Place the 10 objects face-down on the Pyramid, and then scramble them. Put one object in each chamber of the pyramid.

2. Players take turns flipping over objects. A round of play ends in one of two ways:

  ※ A player flips over the Booby Trap. This player scores 0 for the round. The other player scores the total number of artifacts that are flipped over. (If the Booby Trap appears on the first flip, both players score 0.) **Example:** Player 1 flips over the Booby Trap on the fifth turn. Player 1 scores 0. Player 2 scores 4.

  ※ Before the Booby Trap appears, a player chooses not to draw. Both players score the number of objects that they flipped over. **Example:** Player 2 calls it quits on the sixth turn. Player 1 scores 3 points. Player 2 scores 2 points.

3. To begin a new round, turn all the artifacts face-down and scramble them. Place each one randomly on the Pyramid. The player who went first in the last round goes second in the new round.

4. The player with the most points after 10 rounds wins the game.

MATH STRATEGY TIP Player 1 picks first on odd-numbered rounds. Player 2 picks first on even-numbered rounds. Know when the odds are against you and quit while you're ahead. Don't take risks unless you have to.

Booby Trap!
Egyptian Artifacts

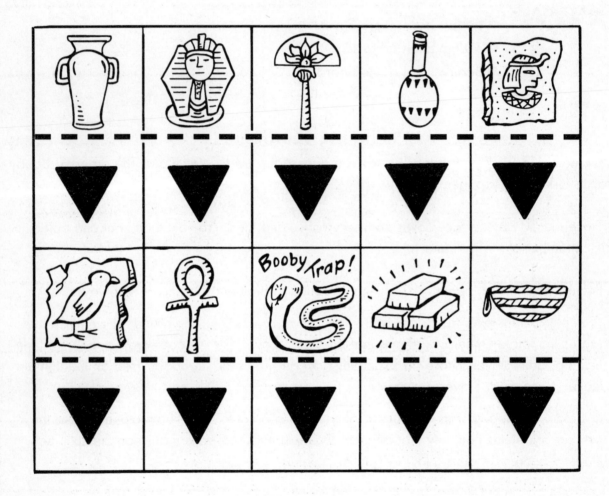

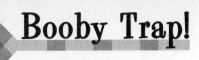

20 Booby Trap!

Score Sheet

Round	Player 1:_____	Player 2:_____
!		
2		
3		
4		
5		
6		
7		
8		
9		
10		

Total: _____   **Total:** _____

Booby Trap!

Game Board

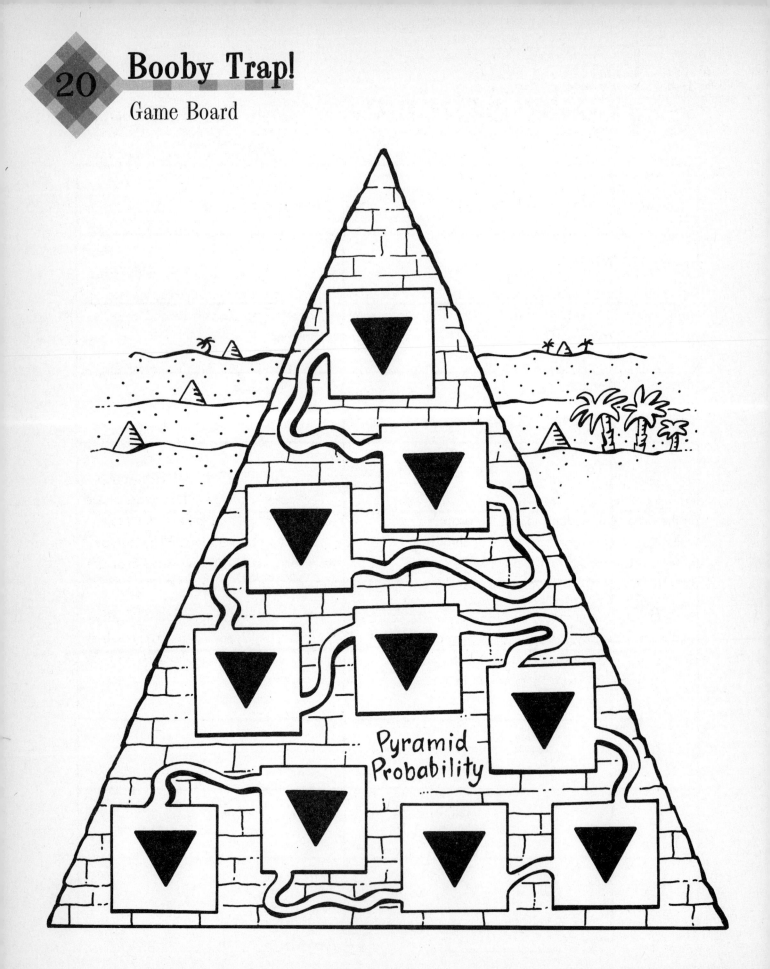

Pyramid
Probability

Players use probability and data analysis to predict the color of the object drawn from a bag.

SKILLS
Probability, graphing, gathering and analyzing data, making predictions, ratios

PREPARATION
Each playing group will need 2 or 3 place markers, a copy of the rules (page 94), one Color Scheme game board per game (page 95), a pen, scrap paper (for keeping score), a bag or box (for a blind drawing) containing 6 counters—3 of one color, 2 of a second color, and 1 of a third color. Use two game boards for more than 3 players.

Write the three colors of the counters on the game board before copying it. Don't disclose the ratio of counters in the bag before playing; discovering this ratio is part of the game.

Basic Math Skills

Ask students to look around the room at the color of shirts (or dresses) that people are wearing. What's the most popular color (blue, black, mixed, and so on)? Make a bar graph of colors based on the data. Ask students to use the graph to make a prediction: Suppose a student is about to walk into the classroom. What color shirt or dress is he or she likely to be wearing? Why do you think so? (The most popular color is the most likely, but there's no guarantee.) How would their predictions change if the next person to walk in were a teacher? a boy versus a girl?

The Color Scheme game is a simple way to make predictions based on the data gathered. The longer students play, the more data they have, and the better their predictions will be. The result of every game is a bar graph. Compare bar graphs for several games (the more, the better), and ask students to predict the ratio of colors in the bag.

Skill Challenge
● Change the ratio of counters in the bag.

Color Scheme

**Players: 2 or 3 or more (use two game
boards for more than 3 players)**

SKILLS Probability, graphing, gathering and analyzing data, making predictions, ratios

MATERIALS
- 2 or 3 place markers (one for each player)
- Color Scheme game board (one per game)
- pen or marker
- scrap paper (for keeping score)
- bag of counters: DO NOT peek inside!

Playing the Game

Which color counter will you draw from the bag next? The player who makes the best predictions wins the game.

1. To start, each player puts a place marker on the first circle of any one of the three color bars. If two or three players choose the same color, stack or group the place markers on the circle.

2. A player draws one counter from the bag. (Players can take turns drawing counters.) Look at the color.

3. Players whose markers are on the color of the counter score 1 point. Keep score on scrap paper. Using a pen or marker, fill in the first circle of this color bar. Then place the counter back in the bag.

4. To begin a new round, players again place their markers on any color bar. Always place your marker on the lowest empty (uncolored) circle of the color bar. A player shakes the bag and draws a counter. Again, score 1 point if you predicted the color of the counter.

5. The game ends when one of the color bars reaches 10. The player with the highest score wins.

VARIATION Players use two place markers instead of one. They can split the markers between two color bars or put them both on the same bar. The maximum score per player per round is 2.

MATH STRATEGY TIP Can you guess the ratio of colors in the bag?

Color Scheme

Game Board

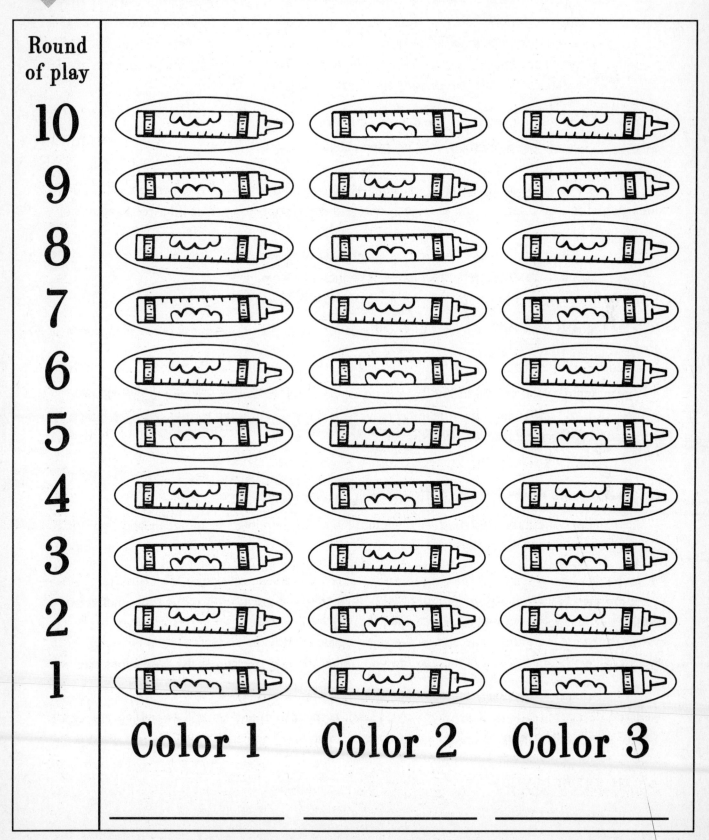

Round of play

10
9
8
7
6
5
4
3
2
1

Color 1   Color 2   Color 3

22 Probability on Ice

Players "perform" skating feats of varying degrees of difficulty by randomly drawing counters from a bag. The color of the counter drawn indicates the results of the "performance" (perfect trick or fall). The higher the level of difficulty, the greater the possible score, but also the greater the risk of "falling."

SKILLS
Calculating probability, making predictions

PREPARATION
Locate 15 uniform counters—9 of one color and 6 of another color. Cut out the three bag labels on page 97 and glue each one to a small paper bag. Place the counters inside the bags as follows:

> Bag 1: 4 counters of Color 1, 1 counter of Color 2
> Bag 2: 3 counters of Color 1, 2 counters of Color 2
> Bag 3: 2 counters of Color 1, 3 counters of Color 2

Color 1 stands for a Perfect Trick. Color 2 stands for a Fall. Write in your two colors in step 4 of the rules (page 98).

Each playing group will need the three bags of counters, a Probability on Ice game board (page 100), a 16th counter (for deciding moves), a copy of the rules (pages 98–99), scrap paper, and a place marker for each player.

Basic Math Skills

Show students the three bags and tell them that there are 5 counters inside each bag, but don't disclose the colors of the counters. Ask a volunteer to draw a counter from Bag 1, write its color on the board, and replace the counter in the bag. Repeat for a total of 10 drawings.

Analyze the results: Based on the data, how many colors of objects are in the bag? Are there equal numbers of colors? Predict: What will probably be the color of the next counter drawn? Why? Make 10 more drawings and further analyze the data. Can students predict the colors of the 5 counters? Point out that the more data you gather, the more accurate the predictions can be.

After playing the Probability on Ice game, discuss students' strategies. How much of the game is luck and how much is skill? (Only the Skater's Choice spaces depend on skill—deciding the wisest degree of difficulty to choose.) Does choosing an easy trick guarantee a point? (No, it is more probable that you will win 1 point, but it is not definite.)

What are the advantages and disadvantages of choosing a Level 3 trick? How does choosing combination moves (doing two tricks in a row) change the odds of falling? (There's a greater risk of scoring 0, but also a greater chance of earning extra points.) Why is choosing a Level 1 combination move not the best move? (1 multiplied by 2 or 3 doesn't increase the score.) How do the odds and scoring change for playing in pairs? (If both players make a perfect move, the score doesn't just double; it triples.)

Skill Challenge

● Students can play a solitaire version of Probability on Ice. Have them create a skating routine by listing any 10 tricks shown on the bags. (It's okay to do the same trick more than once.) What's the best possible score they could earn? Is everyone's best possible score the same? (Higher difficulty means a higher possible score.) Have students draw the results of their routine from the bags. How close are they to perfection? Is it better for a figure skater to do a hard routine or an easy one? Why?

Level 1 Feats

Figure 8   Spiral
Single Jump   Spread-Eagle

(1 point)

Level 2 Feats

Fancy Footwork   Sit Spin
Double Jump   Camel Spin

(2 points)

Level 3 Feats

Triple Jump
Biellmann spin

(3 points)

Bag Labels: Cut out and glue a label on each bag.

Probability on Ice

Players: 1 or 2 to 4; individuals or pairs

SKILLS Calculating probability, making predictions

MATERIALS
- Probability on Ice game board
- 3 bags of counters
- 1 counter
- 1 to 4 place markers (one for each player)
- scrap paper (for keeping score)

Playing the Game

To score points, "perform" figure skating feats—some easy and some\hard. The harder the feat, the greater your possible score. But you also have a greater risk of "falling."

1. Place all place markers on "START."

2. To take a turn, the player to your left hides a counter in either hand. Choose that player's right or left hand. If the hand contains the counter, move your marker 2 spaces. If the hand does not contain the counter, move 1 space.

3. Most spaces describe a skating feat. Each feat is either easy (Level 1), medium (Level 2), or hard (Level 3). If you land on a "Skater's Choice," choose any level of skill from 1 to 3. Harder skills are worth more points, but you have a greater chance of "falling" and scoring 0.

4. To perform a feat, find the bag that matches the level of difficulty. Without looking, choose one counter from the bag. The color stands for the results of your performance.

Color _____ **= Perfect Trick**

Color _____ **= Fall**

If you do a perfect trick, score the number of points equal to the level of difficulty (2 points for a Level 2 trick, for example). Score 0 points if you fall.

Probability on Ice

Players: 1 or 2 to 4; individuals or pairs

5. If you land on an "Artistic Bonus" space, you earn 2 points automatically. If you land on the "Rough Ice" space, you lose 2 points automatically.

6. The first player to reach "END" and finish the routine earns 2 points for speed. The player who finishes with the most points wins the game.

Advanced Rules for Playing

Combination Moves: When you land on a "Skater's Choice," try a combination move. That's two tricks of the same or different levels of difficulty in a row. If you fall on either or both tricks, you score 0. If you make the tricks, multiply the levels of difficulty and add the total to your score.

Example: You choose to do a combination of a double jump (2) and a triple jump (3). You draw a counter from Bag 2 and a counter from Bag 3. If both counters represent perfect tricks, you score 6 points (2 x 3).

Pairs: Team up with a friend and, together, move one game marker around the ice. You both perform each trick by choosing a counter from the bag. Remember to place the first drawn counter back into the bag before the second person draws. If both players fall, score 0. If one player does a perfect trick, add the level of difficulty to your score (1 point for a Level 1 trick, for example).

If both players do a perfect trick, multiply the level of difficulty by 3 (3 points for a Level 1 trick, 6 points for a Level 2 trick, and 9 points for a Level 3 trick).

MATH STRATEGY TIP When you have a choice, don't choose a higher level of difficulty than you need to win. If you're behind, try a Level 2 or 3 combination jump to catch up. (Why won't a Level 1 combo jump help you?)

22

Probability on Ice

Game Board

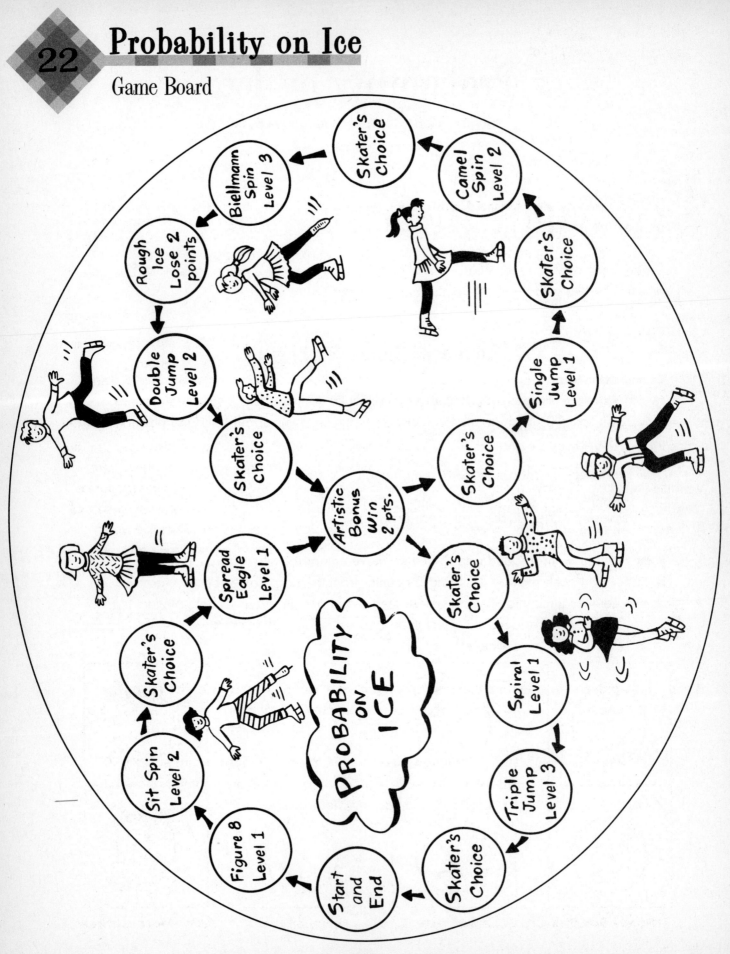

GAME 23 Happy Go Logic

Players: 2 to 4, plus a dealer

Players use logic to decide whether the flip side of a disk is happy or sad.

SKILLS Logical thinking, probability

PREPARATION Provide each playing group with a game board (page 103), 3 disks (cut out and laminate them), 2–4 place markers, a copy of rules (page 102), and a jester place marker.

Basic Math Skills

Mathematical thinking involves looking for patterns among numbers, data, visual shapes, or other information. In Happy Go Logic, the sooner students see the pattern (two disks with like sides and one with opposite sides—happy–happy, sad–sad, happy–sad), the more likely they are to win. At the same time, luck still plays a part. If students have played any of the probability and statistics games (Chapter 6), encourage them to analyze the odds of winning. What are the odds of winning by making random guesses? (They have a 50-50 chance of being right on each guess. Since the Jester advances each time they are wrong, they will probobly end up in a tie in a one-on-one game.)

Skill Challenge

● Add three straight-faced disks to the game. On the backs of these disks, draw a happy face, a sad face, and a straight face. To predict a straight face, students simply say, "Ho hum."

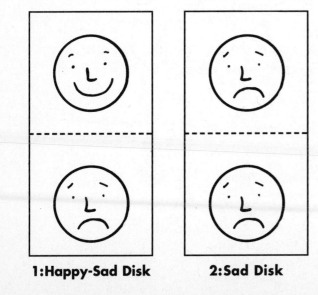

1:Happy-Sad Disk   **2:Sad Disk**   **3:Happy Disk**   **Jester Place Marker**

Happy Go Logic

Players: 2 to 4, plus a dealer

SKILLS Logical thinking, probability

MATERIALS
- Happy Go Logic game board
- 3 disks
- 2 to 4 place markers (one for each player)
- Jester place marker

Playing the Game

1. Put all place markers, including the Jester, on the "START SMILING" space.

2. The dealer secretly scrambles the 3 disks and places them on the game board.

3. Each player in turn guesses what's on the down side of the first disk. If you think it's a happy face, say "Ha Ha." If you think it's a sad face, say "Boo Hoo."

4. After everyone has guessed, flip over the first disk. Players advance 1 space for every correct guess. The Jester advances for every incorrect guess as follows:

   ※ Two Players: 2 spaces for each incorrect guess made
   ※ Three or Four Players: 1 space for each incorrect guess made

   Example: Three out of four players make incorrect guesses. The Jester advances 3 spaces. The fourth player, who guessed right, advances 1 space.

5. Each player in turn guesses what's on the down side of the second disk. Again, advance your marker or the Jester for every correct and incorrect guess (see rule 4). Repeat for the third disk.

6. To begin the next round, the dealer picks up, scrambles, and lays down the three disks.

7. To win, everyone must beat the Jester to the "Happy Ending." If the Jester beats even one player, everyone loses.

MATH STRATEGY TIP Look for a pattern in the disks.

23

Happy Go Logic

Game Board

24 Daisy Chain

Players: 2

In this version of the game Nim, players take turns removing daisies from a chain. The player who takes the last daisy loses the game.

SKILLS
Logical thinking, problem-solving strategies

PREPARATION
Photocopy the Daisy Chain Daisies (page 106) onto tag board and ask students to help you cut them out. Each playing group will need a game board (page 107), a copy of the rules (page 105), and a set of daisies.

Basic Math Skills

The game of Nim has dozens of versions, all of which involve taking or not taking the last object in a pile or making/not making the last move on a board, or a similar strategy. To introduce this strategy, divide students into pairs. Place a small pile of counters (11 or 12) between each pair. Each player takes a turn by removing either one or two objects from the pile. The goal is to make the other player pick up the last object.

Tell students to play again and alternate who goes first. Can they discover a winning strategy? (The player who goes first can remove enough toothpicks on each turn to maintain an odd number in the pile, thus ensuring a win.) How would strategies change if players could remove one, two, or three objects? What if there were too many objects to count?

Skill Challenges

● Reverse the goal so that the player who takes the last daisy wins.

Daisy Chain

Players: 2

SKILLS Logical thinking, problem-solving strategies

MATERIALS
- Daisy Chain game board
- 20 Daisy Chain Daisies

Playing the Game

Take turns removing daisies from the chain. Just don't pick the last daisy if you want to win.

1. Arrange the daisies on the board so that every space has at least one daisy. Some spaces will have stacks of more than one daisy. It doesn't matter which spaces.

2. Take turns picking either one or two daisies from any space. You can't pick daisies from different spaces. And you can't pick more than two daisies. You must pick at least one daisy on each turn.

3. When a stack gets down to zero daisies, the chain is broken. The next player must remove all the stacks of daisies from the smaller length of the chain.

   Example: Player 1 removes the last daisy in space 5.

   Player 2 must remove daisies from spaces 1 through 4, the smaller length of the chain.

4. A player might break the chain and leave two equal-sized lengths of chain. The next player can choose which length to remove.

   Example: Space 5 is empty. Player 2 removes the last daisy in the 8th space. That leaves spaces 6 and 7 on one side and spaces 9 and 10 on the other. Player 1 can pick the daisies on either side of the chain break.

5. To win, force the other player to pick the last daisy on the board.

MATH STRATEGY TIP After you decide on a move, don't pick a daisy yet. First, think about what move your opponent can make based on your move. If you still think your strategy is sound, then go ahead and make the move.

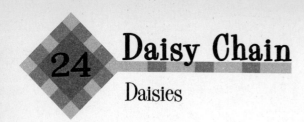

24 Daisy Chain

Daisies

Photocopy onto tag board. Cut out each daisy square.

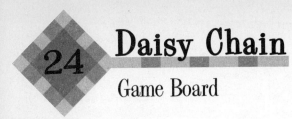

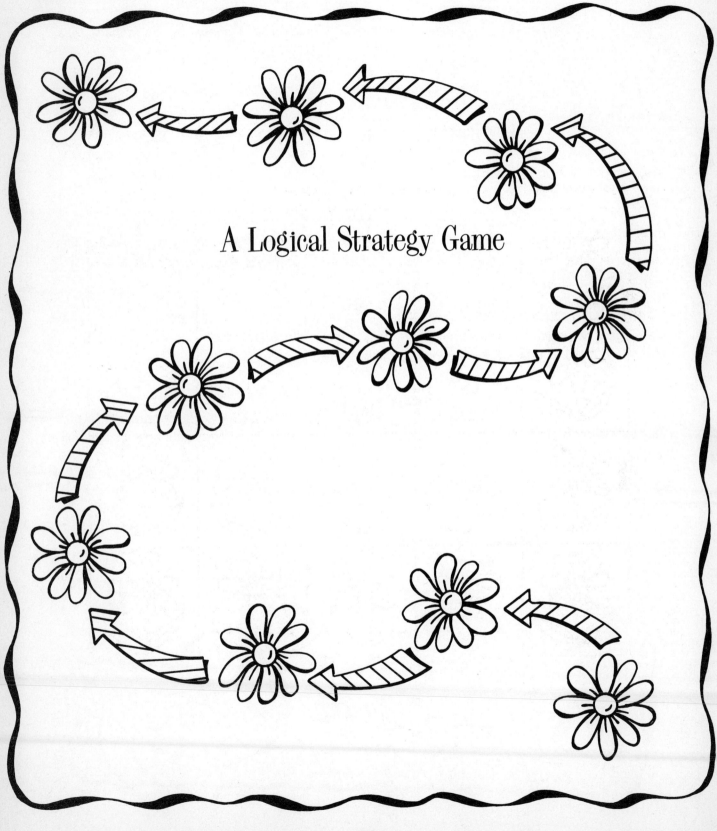

A Logical Strategy Game

Triplets

Players: 1 or 2 to 6 player, plus a dealer/scorer

Players quickly identify sets of objects: three circles, three striped objects, or three spotted objects, for example. The player who identifies the most Triplets (or sets) wins.

SKILLS   Logical thinking, classifying by attributes, visual perception, polygons

PREPARATION   Copy the Triplets cards (page 112) onto tag board. Cut out and laminate them. Each playing group will need a set of cards, a score sheet (page 111), a copy of the rules (pages 109–110), and a pencil.

Basic Skill Review

An attribute is a trait, such as red hair or brown eyes. Ask students to identify attributes that three classmates share. The attributes can include anything from similar clothes to a last name starting with the same letter.

Triplets reinforces a skill vital to both math and science—classification. The attributes in the game are simple: shape (circle, arrow, delta, star, cone, rays), solid versus blank, stripes, and spots. Identifying these attributes amongst a large set of cards can be tricky.

Skill Challenges

● Have students play Anti-Triplets, in which the goal is to identify three cards that have no attributes in common.

● Challenge students to add their own shapes to expand the Triplets deck.

Triplets

Players: 1 or 2 to 6, plus a dealer/scorer

SKILLS Logical thinking, classifying by attributes, visual perception, polygons

MATERIALS
- 24 Triplets cards
- Score sheet

Playing the Game

Match sets of three objects by common attributes (traits): shapes, spots, stripes, and solids.

1. The dealer shuffles the cards well. Then she or he deals the cards from the top of the deck, one card at a time. Place the cards face-up where everyone can see them.

2. Players look for Triplets—three cards that have an attribute (trait) in common. See page 110 for attributes.

3. If you spot a Triplet, say the attribute aloud ("stripes" or "circles," for example). If you are the first to identify a Triplet, you win the cards. In the case of a tie, both players earn points for the set.

4. The dealer deals cards until the deck is exhausted and no Triplets remain.

5. Players score 1 point for each set of three cards that they have won.

6. The dealer shuffles the cards to begin a new round.

7. The winner is the player with the most points after 5 rounds.

ONE-PLAYER RULES Deal the cards face-up, one at a time. When you see a Triplet, pick up the three cards and set them aside. Continue dealing and picking up Triplets until the last card is dealt. Your goal is to match all 24 cards into three-card Triplets. It's not easy! The game depends in part on the luck of the draw.

MATH STRATEGY TIP As the cards are dealt, think of more than one attribute (trait) at a time. Remember the 4 S's—shape, solid, stripe, and spots.

Triplets

**Players: 1 or 2 to 6,
plus a dealer/scorer**

ATTRIBUTES:

Shape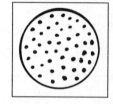

Spots

**Solid or
Blank**

Stripes

Triplets

Score Sheet

Round	Player 1	Player 2	Player 3	Player 4	Player 5	Player 6
1						
2						
3						
4						
5						
TOTAL						

Triplets

Cards

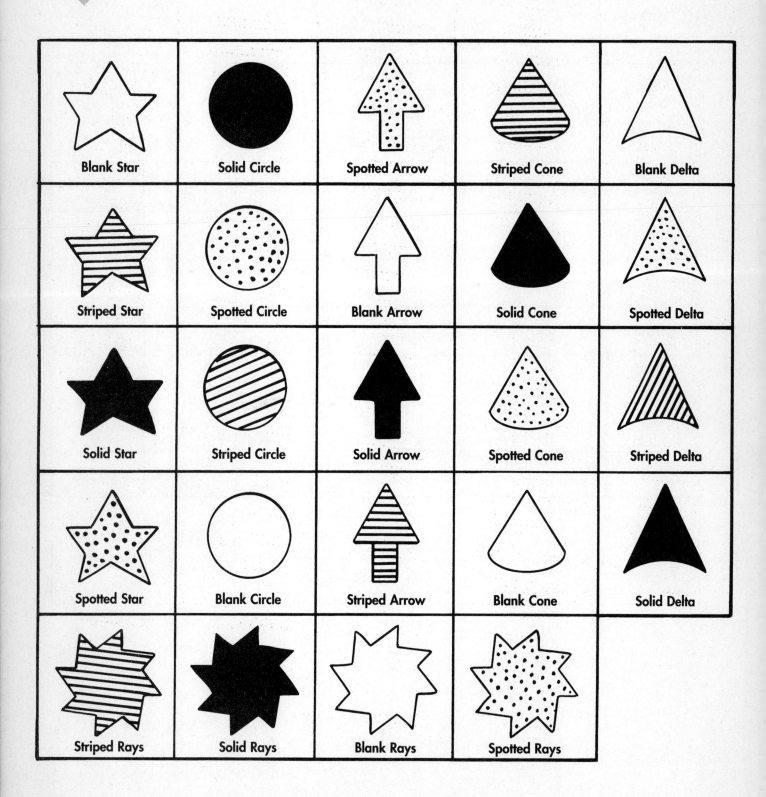

Blank Star	Solid Circle	Spotted Arrow	Striped Cone	Blank Delta
Striped Star	Spotted Circle	Blank Arrow	Solid Cone	Spotted Delta
Solid Star	Striped Circle	Solid Arrow	Spotted Cone	Striped Delta
Spotted Star	Blank Circle	Striped Arrow	Blank Cone	Solid Delta
Striped Rays	Solid Rays	Blank Rays	Spotted Rays	